D0939153

5-9-92

A Prairie Populist

Jane,

I really hope you enjoy
reading Luna Kellie's memoirs.
I was glad to be able to get them
out and published.

Sincerely,

Jane Taylor Nelsen

Singular Lives: The Iowa Series
in North American Autobiography
Albert E. Stone, Series Editor

A PRAIRIE POPULIST

THE MEMOIRS OF LUNA KELLIE

EDITED BY JANE TAYLOR NELSEN

FOREWORD BY ALBERT E. STONE

UNIVERSITY OF IOWA PRESS Ψ IOWA CITY

University of Iowa Press, Iowa City 52242
Copyright © 1992 by the University of Iowa Press
All rights reserved
Printed in the United States of America

Printed on acid-free paper

Library of Congress Cataloging-in-Publication Data
Kellie, Luna.
    A prairie populist: the memoirs of Luna Kellie/
edited by Jane Taylor Nelsen; foreword by Albert E.
Stone.—1st ed.
        p.   cm.—(Singular lives)
    Includes bibliographical references.
    ISBN 0-87745-368-3 (cloth)   ISBN 0-87745-369-1
(paper)
    1. Kellie, Luna. 2. Politicians—Nebraska—
Biography. 3. Populism—Nebraska.
    4. Nebraska—Politics and government. I. Nelsen,
Jane Taylor. II. Title. III. Series.
    F666.K45   1992   91-41361
    978.2'03'092—dc20   CIP

96 95 94 93 92 C 10 9 8 7 6 5 4 3 2 1

96 95 94 93 92 P 10 9 8 7 6 5 4 3 2 1

For my daughter, Madeline Elizabeth,
whose birth added a whole new
dimension to my life and
brought me forever closer to
the experiences of Luna Kellie

★ CONTENTS ★

✯ ACKNOWLEDGMENTS ✯

THIS BOOK evolved from my undergraduate honors thesis, and I would like to thank three advisors who were instrumental in making the thesis possible: Deborah Fink, Linda K. Kerber, and Lauren Rabinovitz. Deborah Fink, by serendipity or fate, steered me toward Luna Kellie as a thesis topic. I had told her I was interested in reform movements, the 1890s, and primary documents, and she suggested I look at Kellie's manuscripts. Deborah also provided me with valuable advice, expertise, and insight on rural women and Populism. As my thesis director, Linda Kerber supported my work at the Nebraska State Historical Society and was always available, despite a hectic schedule, to read drafts and provide helpful, incisive comments. Lauren Rabinovitz originally suggested I write an honors thesis and always provided supportive words and advice at the right moment. I also have Lauren to thank for bringing my work to the attention of Professor Albert E. Stone, who expressed an interest in publishing the memoirs in his Singular Lives series through the University of Iowa Press.

I would like to thank Holly Carver, managing editor of the University of Iowa Press, for her encouraging words and realistic insights and my copy editor, Mary Russell Curran, for her tireless work in pulling the final pieces of the manuscript together. It has been a pleasure to work with both of them. I would also like to thank Al Stone for taking an interest and including this work in his series.

John Schacht, historian and librarian at the University of

Iowa Libraries, was extremely helpful in directing me to source material. In addition, the staff at the Nebraska State Historical Society were always helpful and speedy in providing all the manuscripts and photos needed to complete the project. I thank them for all their assistance.

Special thanks go to my mother, Shirley Taylor Nelsen, who has always encouraged me to be the best that I can be, and to my friends Birgit Grimlund and Laura Ellis, who provided me with encouragement and support. Thanks also go to my father, Carl Nelsen, for his support and interest.

Finally, I would like to thank my husband, John Eiler. Life is a lot easier when you're building on bedrock.

☆ LUNA KELLIE'S MANUSCRIPTS ☆

THE RICHEST source materials I have found on Luna Kellie are held by the Nebraska State Historical Society in Lincoln, Nebraska. They include Kellie's manuscripts, papers, photographs, and letters, as well as issues of Kellie's *Prairie Home* newspaper on microfilm.

In their original form, Kellie's political and personal memoirs were one document, beginning with her account of her "stewardship" of the Farmers' Alliance records and followed by her reminiscences of family life addressed to one of her daughters, Lois Peterson. The 160-page manuscript was handwritten, and I was fascinated to find that the pages are actually old Nebraska Farmers' Alliance certificates. Ornate with red and gold lettering, the certificates must once have been a source of pride for those who owned them. Nearly twenty-four years after Kellie gave up as Alliance secretary, she put the backs of the leftover certificates to good use—with some irony, I imagine.

The date Kellie wrote the original manuscript is uncertain, but after many careful readings of the text I believe it to be 1925. We know from her comments that the text was written after J. T. Kellie's death in 1919, and she often referred to telephones, automobiles, and other contemporary conveniences. Moreover, phrases such as "but now 50 years later" help to pinpoint the date when considered with other dates given in the text.

Kellie's manuscript, along with other Farmers' Alliance records, was transmitted April 21, 1926, to A. E. Sheldon, then superintendent of the Nebraska State Historical Society. At

Page of Luna Kellie's political memoir. Courtesy Nebraska State Historical Society.

some point, Kellie's account of her role as Alliance secretary was typed in a slightly revised form and entitled "The Farmers' Alliance in Nebraska: A History of Its Later Period from 1894 to 1901." Lois Peterson apparently typed her mother's personal memoir separately in May 1975 under the title "Memoirs of Luna Kellie." Readers will notice that it seems unfinished, almost interrupted; in contrast, the ending of the political memoir is all too final.

I have presented the memoirs here in chronological order, starting with Kellie's personal story and adding her major

Sample of the Farmers' Alliance membership certificates on which Luna Kellie wrote her memoirs. Courtesy Nebraska State Historical Society.

speech, "Stand up for Nebraska," ahead of her political memoir. The text appears by and large the way Luna Kellie originally wrote it—in her words and in her unpunctuated style. I have added punctuation and sentence or paragraph breaks only where I believed readers would have considerable difficulty without them. I have also made spelling and capitalization consistent with Kellie's most frequently used forms and have spelled out her few abbreviations. Brackets signal words that are missing or unclear in the original manuscript.

★ FOREWORD ★

Albert E. Stone

LUNA KELLIE of Kearney County, Nebraska, who introduces and recreates herself in these memoirs, is both a representative voice of the majority of American women of her day and a unique historical figure. By writing her autobiography she moved beyond the usual role of inarticulate and obscure farm wife for whom domestic duties and family responsibilities seldom allowed the leisure or inspiration to write more than letters. What made the memoirs possible late in her life was probably her earlier decision to step onto the public stage of Nebraska politics in the 1890s. By becoming secretary of the Nebraska Farmers' Alliance and then publisher of the *Prairie Home* newspaper, Kellie found her public voice and place in the ferment of Populist protest sweeping the Midwest and South during the last decades of the nineteenth century. Less well known, then and now, than "Sockless" Jerry Simpson or Mary Elizabeth Lease (familiar to generations of American history students for her battle cry, "What you farmers need to do is raise less corn, and more Hell"), Luna Kellie enjoyed her moment of public glory when her Alliance address "Stand up for Nebraska" was widely praised and reprinted.

This impassioned speech and poem, which here serve to link Kellie's personal and political memoirs, by no means constitute the chief value of *A Prairie Populist: The Memoirs of Luna Kellie*. To define this life in conventional historical and political terms as valuable because it fits essentially male notions of what events and which institutions really matter is to betray both

Luna Kellie and the millions of other women who have, in fact, played vital roles in creating what Deborah Fink calls "a sustainable society in which people can grow, share lives with loved ones, and do what gives meaning to their lives" (*Open Country Iowa: Rural Women, Tradition, and Change*, p. 3). In recapturing her experiences on the Nebraska prairie, Kellie specifies and dramatizes a profoundly simple fact: farm women like her were at once pioneer travelers, workers, wives and mothers, educators and caregivers, and cocreators with men of a social order that both supported and both came to criticize for betraying their dreams of a better life. While she and her family embraced the common hope of free land and life on the sod-house frontier, they also came to grips with obdurate realities: economic exploitation by railroads and banks, political manipulation by both major parties. Consequently, *A Prairie Populist* exemplifies and extends a feminist rural history based, as Fink argues, on the belief that "women have been major participants [in social, economic, and cultural processes] and have stories to tell that will clarify events shaping rural life and making it distinctive" (p. 7).

To be sure, Luna Kellie never presents herself in modern feminist terms. She is no opponent of patriarchy or of its modes of controlling the destinies of women and children. Marriage and motherhood, unremitting manual labor in field and kitchen, and a usually cheerful acceptance of men like J.T., her husband, mark the years and actions covered by this narrative. Voluntarily restricting herself to the horizon of the sod house, fields, neighborhoods, and towns, she suffers and survives a remarkable range of hardships and deprivations. Just as significantly, she recalls intense moments of joyful fulfillment. No matter how many stories of Willa Cather, Hamlin Garland, Mari Sandoz, or Laura Ingalls Wilder one has read, few of these fictional accounts of frontier farm life can outstrip in honesty, horror, and exhilaration this often ungrammatical and sometimes disjointed narrative.

One typical example of the amateur author's artistry is her account of a midnight race through a pitch-black Nebraska night, over an unfamiliar track behind a pair of horses she had never driven before and had incorrectly harnessed, to bring her father to the bedside of her gravely sick husband. In a totally different mood is an equally typical reminiscence of a summer evening during the Kellies' first months in their sod house:

> As we had no kerosene nor fat enough to make a light with a rag as many did (what they called a slut) I would get the table set out by the south door where the light would strike it and gather old corn stalks and old grass, anything that would make a light fire. Then having set the table with such green stuff as I could gather from the garden as soon as he came I would light the fire and make the shorts [into] pancake and we would sit in the moonlight and eat our supper.

Neither ignored nor bewailed here is the dire poverty of the couple's early married years or their struggle against weather, grasshoppers, fires, crop failures, and diseases of animals and family. What nearly overwhelms Kellie's normally resilient spirits are the deaths of two children, with the after-sting of recalling that some neighbors attended the funerals out of cool curiosity. Against such outsiders' callousness she sets many more memories of the dear friends and loving family members who made up the inner circle of her rich emotional life. Indeed, *A Prairie Populist* is most convincing as a record of a woman's complex feelings and perceptions during a key period in her and her community's past.

As present-day feminist rural historians like Deborah Fink, John Mack Faragher, Lillian Schlissel, Glenda Riley, Judy Lensink, Ann Oakley, and Joan Jensen have variously argued, personal histories like this one must be understood in a dual perspective. If their full cultural significance is to be recognized, readers must carefully trace the specific emotional, social, and material circumstances of a particular life-story. "The material reality of women in a small rural community is significant," Fink declares. "These women struggled to make a living and to create links with each other in order to have some control over their world" (p. 3). Kellie seldom sees herself in her world so sociologically. Yet her personal memoir illustrates a common pattern of rural living and female writing. To trace this pattern also requires an anthropological perspective broader than the individual life's circumstances. This entails stepping back to read the text as an insider's or native's record, freely given, of a changing sociohistorical process. The larger pattern and process governing this microworld is modernization. Therein, Luna Kellie becomes in important respects little different from the Native Americans, silver miners, and cowboys who were also witnesses to their own victimization by a worldwide process of incorporation and centralization. Kellie rides the railroad to her future Nebraska home, whose fate—and hers—is soon to be threatened by the same railroad system.

Her responses to this situation are never simple ones. In her initial self-definition within kinship networks she cheerfully fulfills the roles of worker, helpmeet, childbearer, and food producer. As soon as bare survival is secured, however, Kellie starts serving a broader economic function through her sales of poultry and eggs, some of which reach markets in Denver. When drawn in to the Populist political arena by her husband, she fits with surprising ease into a different world, though one still very much dominated by men. Much of the day-to-day work of the Farmers' Alliance office devolved on her shoulders. Poignant passages record her midnight labors of correspondence and of publishing the *Prairie Home*—unpaid labor carried on with her youngest baby in a box near the desk and all the older children helping mail the newspaper to an ever-shrinking subscription list. The conclusion of her story is equally bleak and graphically contrasts the domestic and political spheres and phases of her past life. After withdrawing from Alliance activities, she sells the printing press that has come to symbolize her role in the farmers' revolt, though the purchaser offered about half what it was worth:

> I gladly took him up and have never written a word for publication to this day. In fact I found myself a physical wreck and it was over 10 years before I had regained my health. . . .
>
> Mr. Kellie who had always urged me to work for the cause saw my condition . . . arranged to begin the much-needed addition to the house which helped occupy my time.
>
> And so I never vote [and] did not for years hardly look

at a political paper. I feel that nothing is likely to be done to benefit the farming class in my lifetime. So I busy myself with my garden and chickens and have given up all hope of making the world any better.

As an autobiographical ending, this passage is a powerfully compressed statement. Throughout the preceding pages, the Kellie homes—their series of sod houses, then a more spacious wooden structure, finally an unfinished addition—represent the core of Luna Kellie's experience and self. If the printing press in one bedroom of the farmhouse represents her later public self, the loss of that press is an apt metaphor for a surrendered but not unforgotten identity and for the agrarian world that gave Luna Kellie her dual self. Through such acts of memory and memoir writing she recovered this lost self.

Personal Memoir

MY FATHER went out to Nebraska in 1875 and filed on a homestead and timber claim and then came back to Wisconsin after his family. My mother having died in 1873, the children were living among relatives, and as he had very little means owing to a series of bad luck over which he had no control he was almost without funds. He agreed with an old friend and neighbor David Richardson of Middleton, Wisconsin, that in exchange for a team of old horses a wagon and some other things I think, so that he could start on his homestead, that as soon as he proved up he would deed 80 acres of the land to him. No papers were made out I think but the bargain was duly carried out of course. Then soon after my marriage he married a young woman about 22 I think and they came out in a wagon in the winter so as to be here for early spring work.

They had unnumbered hardships on the way of which they seldom spoke. There were besides Father and his wife Jennie, Fred, John and little Susie 4 years old. However, before my arrival my father and his wife had parted and she was working in Hastings. Among old letters is one from Brother Fred dated March 10, 1876.

My Dear Sister
I received your letter a short time ago. Our school is out now. I don't know when it will commence again. Our horses are doing well. We have 29 hens and 4 little young chickens. We have 1 cow 1 calf and 2 hogs. We commenced breaking sod 28 day of February. We bought several hundred strawberries and some currants, 50 cherries, 50 plums, 100 apples, 100 peaches. Tuesday all one year old. Paid for in work. Father and Uncle are going to the Republican (river) after a load of little trees to plant on the edge of the field. The place is much different than last year. When we came here first there was no house no barn no nothing and now one year a barn a house 50 acres of land broken and a well. How is the little one? It is snowing and blowing to the other side of Jordan. When it gets through we will go to work and I hope that [will be] soon. We have more snow now than we have had all winter.
F. M. Sanford

My father had written that it would be a good plan to get hold of some more land than we could homestead and that the Union Pacific and B. & M. [rail]roads both had lands near him as the government had given the U.P. every odd section (being ½ the land for 10 miles each side of their track) and the B. & M. lands had to begin outside of that and as he was near the edge we could buy land from either one and the land ticket, as it was called, would apply on the first payment on the land. He said I could come on either road and if on the U.P. [to] get the ticket to Grand Island and if on the B. & M. to Hastings, a new town recently switched in between Juniata and Inland. So we thought he lived somewhere in between the two and as it did not seem to matter your father bought the ticket to Grand Island.

Willie was a little over 5 months old and weighed about 20 and [was] used to having his father toss him around and play with him till he was tired and sleepy. Now when alone and having to sit still in my lap he got very uneasy and I soon became very tired as well as homesick and discouraged, which I had tried to hide from your father as he was about sick over everything anyway. I think we went to Rochelle and had several hours to wait there in a not very nice depot with hard seats so it seemed a relief to get started again. Baby slept pretty good that night and I did the best I could. That was before the days of chair cars and the train was crowded.

There were three coaches of soldiers on the train going out to join Custer I was told and they helped to wile away the time. About every stop a lot of them would jump off onto the platform and greet people and have a jolly time. Poor fellows I often wondered if they joined Custer in time to get all wiped out.

Coming through Iowa there was a young man across the aisle who noticed Willie a good deal, snapping his finger at him etc., and finally he said he knew I must be worn out and to let him romp with him awhile. Willie gladly went to him and he tossed him around and walked around the car with him on his shoulder and a couple of times he got off with him onto the platform. It was a great relief to my arms but my how afraid I was he would kidnap him. Of course I knew there never had been another such a nice baby as no one else ever had such a nice father. But he always gave him back to me and though I never

Luna Elizabeth Kellie, 1892, and James Thompson Kellie, 1890. Courtesy Nebraska State Historical Society.

knew his name or where from or where going I have felt very grateful all my life as I hardly know what I would have done but for him. There were lots of women on board but none came to me and I was too bashful to say anything to them. I had packed lunch enough I thought to see me through but did not feel like eating very much and as Willie had never eaten anything but his mother's milk I did not dare to feed him and he got so hungry because I suppose I did not have milk enough for him. I felt very grateful when the young man bought me a cup of coffee in the morning. Well we got into Omaha finally. I don't know how long since I started but I think 2 days.

We had to cross on a ferry I think. Anyhow we had to change cars and wait some time in the depot and I thought I would eat a little but turned so faint I could not get my valise open. A young German girl about my age but larger and stronger said "Let me open that and take the baby. You look so sick." So she took him and romped with him and I think her mother gave him some milk to drink or something to eat. I felt too bad to know for awhile but took some medicine for my heart and a little to eat. So when the train started my German friends carried my valise and basket and Willie onto the train and the girl sat by me to help hold the baby. The man had been out near Kearney and taken a homestead and built a house and gone back for his family. There were several children, and their kindness made the rest of the journey endurable. How often I wished I could meet them again. I hope they found friends in their time of need which comes to all.

That afternoon it was so hot we had to have some windows open and as the prairie had been burnt over and was all black ashes with a little grass starting we got our clothing and all the car filled with the black soot and it was very very bad. Everyone was warm and sweaty and the black stuck all over us and we all looked terrible. A prim old maid over 40 I am sure sat opposite and she got to looking so funny we could not help laughing.

By and by my young friend made a bed for Willie on her seat and went ahead of her folks to sit awhile. She had hardly got seated when a man above middle age went over by her and went to talking very earnest. I saw she did not like what he said and soon she came back almost in tears and very angry. "The old fool asked me to marry him," she said. "My, what kind of a girl does he think I am." She said he told her he had a homestead near Kearney and a house and how many horses and cows etc. And he could not farm and bake so he needed a wife (he was a widower) and was sure she would suit. Well by the time she was feeling a little better we saw he was talking earnestly to another young woman and soon to another a little older but he was sure persevering so soon he came and sat by the old maid and told her all his story and she smiled very sweetly smutty face and all and soon took her valise and went to the toilet room and stayed quite awhile [and] then came out with a clean waist and fresh curls etc. and went to her seat. He put his arm along the back and she put her head on his shoulder and they both looked as if perfectly happy. But my young friend and I could hardly keep a straight face but had to find some excuse all the time to laugh.

It was nearly sundown when we reached Grand Island and I bade farewell to my kind friends. I was real excited as I was sure my father would be waiting for me and I was so proud to show him my baby. Cab drivers and hotel runners crowded around so I could not see but I told them all no I was waited for. The train pulled out everyone departed and I was alone on the platform where I stayed some time and could not see anyone coming or looking for anyone.

Such an appalling catastrophe had never occurred to me and I did not know what to do. If I went away from the depot I feared my father would come and not find me so I sat around till dark and then asked the agent where was a good cheap hotel. He finally sent a man to me who had a hotel nearby, another German. He took me over to their hotel and said he would keep watch and if anyone came looking for me [he] would call me. His wife was a good motherly woman and took me up to a small but very clean room, the only one left, and told me the town was so full of people crowding in because of the Indian uprising that it had been and was very hard to get a place to stay. I could see the town was crowded and lots camping around. It seemed that all the north part of the state was greatly excited and rushing into the railroad towns. Of course that made me quite uneasy and I wished Father was there. After thinking things over awhile I concluded nothing but severe sickness or death had prevented my father from meeting me. Perhaps he had been waylaid by Indians. I went down to the good landlady and told her I must get someone to take me in the morning on somewhere between there and Hastings to my father's and she had word sent and a man came to see me and agreed to start early in the morning if my father had not arrived and to take me and my trunk as far as Hastings (about 25 miles) for four (4) dollars, if he had to go farther it would be more.

So eating some more cold lunch in the morning we started early [and] went across the river and along a lot of low land willows etc. out 4 or 5 miles I think when we saw a team and lumber wagon coming the horses old and poor but good travellers and the man so haggard and poor we almost passed him but he pulled up and it was Father. He had been breaking prairie on the Blue River fully 70 miles from Grand Island. Mr. O.H. Wright's folks brought out the postal card from town telling him when I would be there. They put a boy on a horse and sent him 25 or 30 miles to take it to my father. It was well toward noon and I would be in Grand Island that night and his team was tired but he unhitched and started and came as far as he could, unhitched and let his horses browse around till morning and started on again. I doubt whether he had either dinner supper or breakfast himself. But he was greatly worried for fear I would be scared and not know what to do. Well the man said give him $2.00 and he would go back which I did and we transferred to the lumber wagon for a 50 mile trip for he lived over 20 miles the other side of Hastings.

It almost broke my heart to see my father look so old and poor and worried besides being so poorly clad and when we got to Hastings which had only 3 or 4 stores I think and only one with dry goods I bought some shirting to make shirts for him and the boys who had been batching. There had been some rain and Hastings seemed to be in a mudhole no sidewalks and altogether the worst looking little town I had ever seen. We got a little lunch to put with mine and jogged on.

The sun was very hot and bright. The prairie had all been burnt and grass just starting [and] not one spear seemed to dare to grow an inch higher than another. Not a tree a shrub or even a gooseberry bush to be seen all the way and not many houses and most of them sod. The first one I saw I said "But it is most black." Pa said "What color did you think a sod house would be?" "Oh nice and green and grassy" I said "not such a dirty looking thing." "Well" he said "it is dirty looking because it is made of dirt." Really I had thought a sod house would be kind of nice but the sight of the first one sickened me. The bright sun in our faces soon gave me a terrific headache which is the most I remember of the ride except there was hardly anything to call a road. We went down all the little ditches and up again, no culverts or anything. I was so frighted I thought I would stay still when I got there.

Just before dark we got to Aunt Hattie's where Sister Susie was staying and of course I was delighted to see her and her to see the baby. I should have said his Grandpa was so delighted with him he would not let me hold him but gave him the end of the line to drive with.

After a good supper at Aunt Hattie's we started on taking Susie with us but leaving the spring seat which pa had borrowed for the occasion and as the sun was down the journey was better except we now had no road but took cross lots across cottonwood creek and several gullies which kept me scared as the old team always seemed to try to run away. One was a blackhawk horse Pa brought from Wisconsin, the other one a gray about the same spirit. With little or no grain and working hard every day they never got their spirit broken but always wanted to run. We finally reached home where brother Fred was batching but John was working for a neighbor. Fred was 14 at this time and slender and rather small for his age, John 11 and short and strong. Fred was certainly glad to see me and baby, though boylike he did not say much but romped with baby. But I was too exhausted to look around or even to talk so we went right to bed.

A word as to how Father came to Nebraska. In the summer of 1871 Father was working on the Northern Pacific R.R. and we were living in a rented house in the village of Lansing, Minnesota. Mother got hold of some literature sent out by the B. & M. R.R. telling of the glories of Nebraska and how there were homesteads to be taken within 4 miles of the State Capitol and the University. She was greatly enthused and as Father came home that fall she read it all to him and urged him to go and as we say now and "get in the ground floor." He very sensibly told her he had absolutely nothing to start on except one team and wagon but she still urged him to put our household goods in the wagon and start out before all the homesteads close to the Capitol were taken.

This was a very odd thing as she always was opposed to moving and would rather stay most anyplace than to have to move. But Father had taken her to one new country when they were first married (Minnesota where I was born) and he knew she was not built for a pioneer and how she nearly died with homesickness, and winter coming on and all he stood firm not to go. His brother Joseph was visiting us then and he sided with Mother and said he would buy another team so they could take more stuff and he would go with us and together they would find something to do and get along. But one day Father came in and said he had rented a farm near there and was going to move onto it and start plowing right away.

As most young folk would be I was greatly disappointed. It seemed to me a great chance to see a beautiful country like the pictures showed and have a lot of thrilling adventures. Besides I hoped in a few years to go to a University and it would be so nice to have it near home.

Well 2 years of farming bankrupted Father so we moved off the farm without even a team. Spent the hard winter of '72 and '73 in Austin where Father worked in a roundhouse and developed a bad cough from his old army wound and in February or March he went South to St. Louis and went to work on a R.R. bridge gang of which Mr. Kellie was foreman. He sent for us in April and we spent the summer on the east bank of the Mississippi nearly opposite the old Jefferson Barracks. It was very unhealthy and very hot and misty. Everyone around us had the ague and expected to have it. Mother held off until fall [and] then got the malarial Typhoid and died.

Father had such bitter regrets that he had not come to Nebraska when she wanted to where whatever hardships she might have to have undergone the climate was so healthy she would likely have lived to raise the family. [It] made him take the first opportunity to move there.

The glowing accounts of the golden west sent out by the R.R. company remained in my mind and I had a vague idea being only 14 years old that they were doing a noble work to let poor people know there was such a grand haven they could reach. It was quite a number of years afterwards that I saw a statement in a Boston paper from one of the R.R. officials saying how profitable the advertising had been and that they estimated that they had cleared $1500 from each emigrant they had obtained. Well that was a low estimate I know now though I did not see it even at the time, for the minute you crossed the Missouri River your fate both soul and body was in their hands. What you should eat and drink, what you should wear, everything was in their hands and they robbed us of all we produced except enough to keep body and soul together and many many times not that as too many of the early settlers filled early graves on account of being ill nourished and ill clad while the wealth they produced was being coldly calculated as paying so much per head. But more of that later as it was many years before the situation became clear to us and I am glad of it for during those years we had youth and *hope* which means happiness and we worked ourselves harder than slaves were ever worked to be able to fulfill our hopes.

When I think back now to the little girl I really was when I came to Nebraska not quite 19 years old with a dearly loved husband left behind and a bright healthy baby boy who lived entirely on his mother's milk, it does not seem strange that I was unnaturally homesick and nothing around seemed good to me. Of course I was very glad to see my father and brothers and sister again but to see them in such wretched circumstances made me heartsick indeed and I would not go to any of the neighbors' for some time and felt most wretched when any of them came there as I could not realize that they were no better off and indeed many of them not nearly so well off as we were. For instance our dugout had two rooms and I had the inner one which was as private as need be while many perhaps most of the sod houses only had one room. Then we had a very good cave by the house and many things were kept in it that others had to crowd in their one room. Then our roof did not leak and most of them did but Father had used large logs in the roof so he was able to pile on enough dirt to keep it from leaking which most of them could not do, but I did not realize any of these blessings until time had gone on and I was deprived of them.

The dugout was made by digging out the ground the same as for a cellar. Ours was down about 3 feet in the ground, then sod [was] laid in a wall about 2 feet thick and 3½ feet high and it was plastered with mud on the inside walls and the dirt floor was levelled down pretty good and pounded down quite hard. But oh what a place, I thought, for a baby just beginning to creep and no dresses but white ones.

The gable end of our (rather my father's) dugout was in the south and a real window of 2-sash 8 x 10 lights was in the south and really did make it quite light and a nice deep windowsill but I did not appreciate that until a good deal later [when] I realized most of the settlers only had 1 sash. There was only 1 sash in the inner room and it was high in the peak as it was farther in the ground so [there] was not room for more but it gave good ventilation.

It was not hard to get ventilation those days. It seemed to be always blowing some way. I had kept close in the house all winter and now the awful wind made me feel I never wanted to go out of doors. It seemed to blow from the north until it was blown out and then turn around and blow it all back again. The others did not seem to mind it but it was a real misery to me and I hardly seemed that first summer to get the real charm of the Prairie at all.

Pa did not have any oxen of his own but a neighbor about 6 miles off let him take a team of old and large bulls to work for their keep and Fred was breaking prairie with them on the south or Richardson 80. They were quite [wild] when not yoked up and one of them had to be yoked first and unyoked last as the other one would not stand alone with the yoke on. I don't see now how Fred young and light as he was ever handled the brutes but he always had a great way with stock and they got along all right but [for] one day either beginning of harvest or haying [when] Pa was going to work for O.H. Wright as he had no harvest of his own and wanted Fred to go with him. He was going to let the oxen stay still on their lariat ropes but Johnny said he could handle them and they helped him get yoked up and went away.

He let them browse with the yoke on while he came to dinner but [later] it came quite dark. I had supper ready and John did not come. I was afraid he was hurt so took Willie who was a heavy boy at least 25 pounds and walked down to the breaking and found Johnny all right and he was just going to unyoke and lariat the oxen on the unbroken land. Of course I told him just about crying how frighted I had been and asked why he had not come before. "Oh he just wanted to go a round more than Fred had been going" and he had so he started to unyoke and took the bow off the wrong bull first. John hollered "Run for the house Lou run" and I surely ran. No sooner did the one bull find the weight of the yoke all on his neck than he jumped in the air and ran and bawled and tossed the yoke from side to side and bawled and jumped and bawled and John with the whip tried to keep him from going toward the house which he seemed possessed to do. I should say that all the way down there I had been scared for fear there were rattlesnakes in the grass so I was trembling with fear when I got there but going back I did not think of snakes but could hear that awful bellering behind me. But I ran even with the heavy baby. I got over the ground as lively as I ever made nearly ½ mile I think for I could hear that in spite of John's efforts the bull was coming my way. John would seem to head him with the whip but he would dodge by and I suppose he may have wanted water at the well but anyway when I reached the dugout he was not far behind still jumping and bellering. He tore around there till the other got loose and came too and they ran and bellered and fought on all sides of the house so I sat with Willie in my arms too exhausted to move and expected every minute they would get on the roof (which was even with the ground on the north end) and break through the roof. But after a while Pa and Fred came and they managed some way to get them back on their ropes but it was real late before Johnny and I could eat any supper and I for one was too exhausted and shaking to eat much.

Pa and Fred had worked until dark then went in and had supper then drove 3 or 4 miles home. After that they let the breaking go and John went to the harvest field with the others. As they did not want to ask me to stay alone they drove back and forth night and morning which made them get up much earlier and get to bed later but they did not complain.

The days seemed very long with just Susie 5 years old and baby and I. There was nothing to read. There were few weeds in the garden on the new sod and no material to sew, only some patching. When it began to get dark we used to go and sit on the cave where we could see all around and the little owls used to hoot so lonesome and sometime the coyotes would howl, and I used to be sure at times it was Indians signalling to one another off in the sand hills south and west of us for there were no houses in sight and it seemed like the end of the world. But most every night when we sat alone some little antelopes would come and look at us with great curiosity and come a little nearer and nearer till sometimes they got real close just a few rods but they always went away before Pa and the boys came. They were pretty and graceful little things and they seemed to want to know us but as soon as the wagon rattled in the distance, a flash, and they were gone. I never can hear a coyote or hoot owl now without seeming to see a picture of us there grouped on top of the cave because we were afraid to stay in the house as it had only one outside door and if Indians or anything came in that door we could not get away. So though sometimes the nights were chilly we wrapped something around us and cuddled close together and I kept close watch and listened for the least noise, for I had the idea that out there if Indians came we might run and hide out in the corn or grass and not be caught in a trap.

Well there were no Indians anywhere around and I did not see one for 20 years when I saw one at the depot in Omaha but the fear was as dreadful to me as if they were really there and I guess no one knew for sure but they might be. For that was the summer of the Custer massacre and the plains Indians were all off their regular hunting grounds.

Callers

The first Sunday the boys had a visitor young Clarence Griswold who was a year or so older than Fred who stayed to dinner which embarrassed me a good deal as I did not think our dinner good enough for company but he evidently did as he came again the next Sunday and the next and about every Sunday all summer until I got used to his coming in with the boys. He was the head of the family at that time as his father, an old soldier, was fortune hunting in the Black Hills of South Dakota and Father thought him a model boy to stay and work so faithfully and hard all week for his mother and 3 sisters and they had so little to do with. They had hauled a little wood up from the Blue the winter before but whenever they wanted to chop a little had to come and borrow an ax. Also hammer and pieces of harness etc. etc. Father did all he could to show him how to mend things and get along and as their were no other boys for some miles around I suppose the Sundays he spent with the boys were really quit a treat to him. No doubt looked forward to all week. His mother never came to see me but the 2 oldest girls did and I well remember them in their clean starched calico dresses and sun bonnets [and] barefooted which seemed strange to me then. But they were sociable and well–read girls about 15 and I liked to have them come which was not very often.

Then one forenoon came a widow woman whose land cornered ours. My father had told me about her coming out to talk to him as he passed there to the Blacksmith shop and to go to his timber claim. She tried to be very sociable and had travelled a great deal, had been to college when young and quite well off. She stayed to dinner but I did not ask her back and never returned her call.

That was the extent of the callers that summer except [for] Mrs. Buss a distant relative by marriage whom I was delighted to see and made a confidant of, urging her to come often. Afterwards Father said she told him I did not ask her and he was angry till I explained. That was my first experience with a liar and although he made me return her call I never went again. That was a bitter experience as I had thought to find a friend and it took me a long time to understand or get over it. When father and the boys were to be gone a few days harvesting he got her daughter Ida to come and stay with me. We had nothing to do except cook a little for ourselves so I busied myself to finish a fine quilt I had about ⅓ made before marriage. It was a log cabin of fine material Aunt Sophy and Susie had given me and I had abundance of pieces for at least 2 quilts. She was a winning girl and confided to me that she was to be married in a few months and finally proposed to take the quilt home and finish it [in exchange] for enough of the pieces to make her one. I was not very willing but she was so taken with the fine pieces and I finally let her take them, she assuring me her mother and sisters would help her and I would soon have my quilt finished. Well she got married and I did not like to remind her of the quilt but finally at church I noticed her baby wrapped in a small quilt I knew I had pieced myself. So she promised again and again to bring the pieces to church when I could get them but years ran on and she did not do so and at last I went to her house for them. There was the baby quilt soiled and pretty well worn, 2 or three chair cushions also worn. The babies had on little sacques and skirts made from the larger pieces, and in short all she seemed to find was a small handful of pieces for me.

This was another shock to me. I had not realized as I do now that a lying mother will most surely raise liars and thieves. I have often told young mothers when I hear them telling babies the "black man" or "a bear will get you," "How will you like it when they lie to you as they will after your many lessons?"

Brothers Fred and John were so delighted to have a baby boy around they could hardly leave him to go to their work but whatever they could do with one hand was done with him in their arms. The fact that he liked rough boys' play made him dearer and they seemed to think he was the nicest thing ever happened in their lives. If one of them could carry him and I would come out and look at each little tree or bush they had planted (for they loved them all) their happiness knew no bounds. But while I tried to be interested and not dampen their ardor I secretly felt that it would be so long before those slender little whips could bear any fruit, so long to wait it hardly was worthwhile. For you see I was so homesick for my lover husband everything was seen through blue glasses. But now 50 years after I have set out a number of such little whips in which I take great pride and delight and think although I may never gather their fruit, while I am waiting I may as well have the fun of seeing them grow.

The boys were so anxious for me to like their country they drew my attention to the meadow lark with its beautiful song and brought me every little kind of wild flower they could find and soon began to take me where the prairie was literally covered with beautiful buffalo peas, really the most lovely sight I had ever seen.

But my father's pride and joy in his grandson even surpassed that of the boys and they as well as myself had very little of him when he was around, and in breaking 10 acres on our railroad land across the road from him (which I had turned in my R.R. ticket on and J.T. paid him to break) he had Willie ride on the plow several trips a day and begrudged him the time in which he ate and took his naps. And in putting up hay he always took him with him and when they came up with a load would jump off and run to the house with him and call "Here Lou take this boy and feed him while we pitch off this load." And [he] never failed when the load was off to come after him and when he went to sleep with him he would wrap him up in his old coat he carried with him on purpose.

Father and the boys worked very hard the winter before

hauling up logs from the Blue for fuel and we had the largest woodpile I ever saw in Nebraska but it had cost lots of long hard days' work in the cold to get it. Father was a fine axman and part of it he had paid for by cutting timbers on shares. So we had plenty of good fuel which few had and I was to appreciate later. But among those not so fortunate was T. B. Burns an old soldier and great friend of Father's who had only come on that spring and I do not think had a team. They lived between Father's homestead and timber claim so he went by there often and Burns helped him with the hay and Father used his team and put up some for Burns. Mrs. Burns came along in the summer from Pennsylvania and was very homesick. I had never seen her but Father reported her as looking as if she cried all the time and of course everything was very hard for her as she had been used to all the comforts of life. About the first of September it came on a rainy spell and a cold north wind. I got out Willie's flannel clothes and put [them] on him even in our warm house. Father went and looked out several times and still it poured. Finally he said Burnses have nothing to burn but buffalo chips and they won't burn now, and putting on his old coat he went out and hitched up his team and loaded up some wood and took it over. As he had no rubber coat or anything of course he was soaked through before he got there but he came back feeling better and dried out. Said they needed it and Mrs. Burns cried more for joy. Telling me of it many years after she said she had been so homesick she did not like anything or anybody in the country but when Father drove over there soaking wet in that cold wind to bring them some fuel she made up her mind that a country with such neighbors would not be unendurable and was never so homesick afterwards.

One day in the later part of June Pa came home and said he had seen a number of the neighbors and they felt that as it was centennial year they wanted to celebrate and did not have the money to fix up their families to go off to some town celebration and thought they might get together and have a picnic and good time at the Mayflower school house. Said the Spindlers would all come with their band. This was a fife and drum corps. They were civil war drummers and had the best band in the country. They had called a meeting at the school house to appoint committees etc. and he wanted me to go and agree to read the Declaration of Independence. I was [terribly?] schooled, a stranger in a strange land, and to be put forward when I actually could not go at all. I told him I had no clothes. I really did not have a new thing that summer and hat and all must be old-fashioned I knew and to get up before the audience that way I nearly fainted. So he agreed not to have me read but really I must go and get acquainted. There were nice neighbors but they all had to work their teams so hard they did not have much time to visit and the reason they had the celebration there was because none of them had new clothes but felt they wanted to show their patriotism some way. Said he would have to wear his everyday clothes and so would the boys and all the others and as I was the newest comer I would be dressed better than any of the others. O.H. Wright and a number of the young folks were going away I forget where to celebrate and wanted him to go but that would mean new clothes etc. So finally I agreed to go but I sure did dread it.

Pa was on some of the committees and was busy getting things ready. [He] hauled up green willows from sand creek or the Blue for a bower [and] meantime he had gone to town and got a list of things I just had to have to make a good picnic dinner. He must have got the boys a work shirt or so and probably one at least a new pair of overalls but they went barefooted. This worried me a lot but I found out they were just in style. I baked a large pan of light biscuits, roasted one of Pa's few light Brahma hens with lots of dressing, made a large cake with loads of raisins and some kind of pie so I kept busy and had after all my worries a very good dinner.

The day turned out to be a lovely one, the morning bright and fair with only enough breeze for health and pleasure. Uncle Chester and Aunt Hattie drove around our way for us with their lumber wagon and large team. Uncle Chester was an old Veteran Soldier tall and spare with a good-humored twinkle in his eye, Aunt Hattie short and plump with bright dark brown eyes always seeing the funny side of life. No one could be blue or sober long around her. They had some neighbors with them with 2 or 3 little girls and with their 2 boys we had quite a load but I remember when we got up to Griswolds' he got in and went with us. He had just got home from gold hunting in the Black Hills the day before and seemed very glad to get home even without the gold. We realized how fortunate they were to escape being killed by Indians as so many gold seekers were that year. He also was an old Union Soldier. His family did not go with us and I do not think they went unless Clarence may have gone afoot. Mrs. G. was quite timid and seldom went out and I think now she probably thought her clothes were not good enough but I am not sure.

The school house was 2 miles straight north and as the prairie was now covered with bright green grass the beauty of the prairie began to impress me. As we neared the house we could hear the band playing the fifes and drums carrying us all back to old civil war times when the boys came marching home. I don't know where they got all their lumber but I believe Strohls lent a lot they had bought for their new sod house which was large with a sweet potato cellar underneath so it had floor beams and floor besides being quite large had a lot of roof lumber. Perhaps they furnished it all but I think some of the Spindlers lent some. Anyway across the east end of the school house was a bower built probably 12 feet wide and projecting about that far North of the building, also along the North side a bower about 12 feet wide so the speakers' stand and musicians back of it were in the open corner 12-foot space and [there were] seats in both parts of the bower facing the speakers. The whole was well covered with green boughs and was quite artistic as well as practicable.

The eatables were unloaded and carried into the school house and the number of those with babies took in quilts pillows etc. to make them comfortable. I believe Israel Spindler was chairman but forget for sure. Someone read the Declaration of Independence and the band played often. Also we sang often all the old patriotic war songs which we all knew so well. And when we had a recess for dinner with jolly Aunt Hattie to introduce me I forgot my dress was out of date for everyone was pleasant and homelike. No one was dressed up, only all the dresses were clean and neat, and no one seemed to mind how anyone was dressed.

The noon hour was quite informal. Aunt Hattie and her

friend and I spread our dinner on top of some desks and all the desks were occupied in the same way. I remember Pa ran around the room most of the time eating and jollying everyone and showing them his grandson and if they thought there ever was another as nice they better not let him know it. Also he called or brought up some men and boys who did not seem to have women folks there and insisted on feeding them while he sampled other people's cooking. In fact I think most of the men did the same. I know a good many had a piece of my large fruit cake and women also tasted of this and that of the others and all had a jolly good time.

I caught Fred and John feeding Willie fruit cake and protested strongly only to hear "Gee Lou he knows it is good. We have fed him most of our raisins. Sure it won't hurt him [and] the little dickens just loves them." But that night when they heard him crying so much with tummy ache they promised to be more careful. However fruit cakes were not to come soon again.

This was my first acquaintance with Mrs. Strohl, my best friend to be for nearly 50 years, who came nearer being a mother to me than any other in the years to come. She was a tall swarthy Tennessee woman. I had heard that she chewed tobacco and had said "Ugh I never want to know her." But that day she was there with her 4 little girls just a little step apart all dressed in pretty pink muslin just alike with tucks and ruffles and narrow white lace and she so motherly my heart warmed to her at once. While she "tooken a fancy" at once to the young and lonely stranger. So little do outside manners tell of the pure gold in the heart. Without that friendship that day begun I know I must have fainted and dropped by the wayside ere many years had flown.

Among those who had no women folks present was T. B. Burns and C. B. Powers. Mrs. Burns was still in Pennsylvania. He had a sod house built and she soon came. Powers' family were near Lincoln and came on that fall. He ran a blacksmith shop on the corner of his land. Both were old soldiers. In fact I think Old Man Higgins and Charles Buss were the only men present who were not.

The Higgins[es] came with an ox team I remember and the

old lady and 2 or 3 girls might have stepped from bandboxes, so freshly starched were their clothes and so terribly stiff and white their collars and cuffs. And they always seemed to keep that way. But most of them died in a few years with T.B. which was what brought them to Nebraska. There were many present I do not remember for there was a large crowd. All the sod town folks the Halcombs Crones and Swinfords 3 families of Spindlers.

Israel Spindler was the main speaker after dinner. He reviewed the causes of [the] Declaration of Independence and on down, a very good speech. Then my father and others spoke more on the civil war for liberty. Uncle Chester and many others made short speeches on much the same vein. Interesting personal experiences. And during this day Custer's band was being annihilated but we did not hear it for several days. Some of the children had gone to a distance to play games so as not to disturb the speaking and some of the babies were always asleep in the school house but at last the lowering sun forced us to disband and the Centennial Celebration at Mayflower closed with music by the band.

Garden

Although only one year from sod the garden spot where the fruit trees and bushes were planted had by repeated plowing and harrowing been so pulverized that we had a really fine garden with very few weeds. We all took a great interest and pride in it and very soon it made a lot of difference in our table. I then learned as I had not realized before what a difference a few fresh vegetables can make in the appearance of the table as well as the satisfaction of the appetite; and I resolved always to have abundance of them in season and a cellar full for winter, which resolve has been pretty fully carried out to a great advantage both to pocket book and health. I am convinced that nothing else equals an early hour or two in the garden with hoe and rake to keep an *overworked* housewife equal to her duties. She comes back to the dishes and cooking with lungs full of fresh air which could not be got by simply walking or riding around, and the outdoor interest brightens the day, and makes the indoor work more pleasing. I always began to feel more fit in the spring as soon as I could get out to work in the dirt.

While Father and the boys had been off harvesting the year before, the grasshoppers had "lit" where they were at work, and ending all need of work had harvested everything themselves, even the grain already shocked. So the boys were often talking about it and wishing I could have seen them and wondering when they would come again. I had seen a few hoppers I thought all my life and could not realize how they could do all the damage they did in so short a time but one clear afternoon about 3 o'clock Johnny came to the dugout door and hollered "Luna come out here and see the grasshoppers flying over."

I came out and looked around but did not see any hoppers. Looked up and did not see any.

"Why there are no hoppers" I said.

"Yes that cloud is hoppers" said John.

"No that is just a cloud" I said. "See, it is going to rain."

"Yes I am afraid it will rain hoppers" said John. "Can't you see them?"

"No."

"Come here" he said. "Now get the edge of the roof between you and the sun and look."

As I did so I exclaimed "Oh John it is going to snow. The air up there is full of snow, big white flakes of snow. Lots of it is beginning to come down."

"Yes" said John "they are starting to light. What can we do, what can we save? Let us go to the garden and get what we can. We can put some things in the cellar."

And off he ran for [a] box or sack to gather something in. I was slower as I did not see the need to gather green and perishable garden stuff until something was destroying it but by the time I could get out the things were already gray with locusts and the air full of more coming down. They lit on me my head my dress my hands and no place to put my feet except as they hopped up probably onto me. John was frantically pulling young beets and carrots and onions but he shouted to me to go back and try and keep them out of the house. He could save what we could use of the green stuff before it spoiled.

The sweet corn was just getting big enough to begin using

but now no corn could be seen. The green was all covered with gray hoppers and where the ears were was simply a large cluster of hoppers while between the rows they were several hoppers deep waiting for a chance to feed. And the noise. Who could believe a grasshopper feeding made a noise but the whole army of them made a noise as of a bunch of hogs chanking. I was glad to get back in the house but found the entry way well stacked with hoppers so it was hard to shake them off my clothes and get in without a lot of them going in also and I had no desire to go out among them again. They still kept slowly coming down, coming down looking like snow till nearly down they changed to gray. Finally John gave up and came in and we sure felt pretty blue.

"That is the end of all our fruit trees and berries" said John "as well as the corn and potatoes."

"Oh surely they can't eat the potatoes John."

"Well they will eat all the tops and all that are near the top and they are so green they will rot in the ground." John had brought the shovel in the house when he came and I now saw why as he opened the door and went out and shovelled the hoppers out of the entry way to the dugout. This he did every little while and between times he chased and threw out those that had got in the house so he kept pretty busy. and when he went after a bucket of water he took a big cloth to tie over the pail so he could get it home without half hoppers as he said. Night came. Father and Fred came home and we went to bed but could still hear the hoppers chanking chanking.

The next morning the hoppers were still there though the chanking was not so loud as most of the green stuff was eaten. I think that towards night they rose up and left as suddenly as they came though it may have been the morning after.

Anyway when they said they were gone I went out of the house and to the garden to see what was left. Desolation only. Where the onions carrots beets and sweet potatoes had been was not a single thing, no sign of leaf or stem, only holes in the ground where they had eaten down and eaten out every bit of vegetable fiber. The fruit trees had all the small limbs completely eaten away and all the bark from the entire tree and if they had stayed a few hours longer I suppose there would have been only holes in the ground where roots were eaten out. The corn was eaten off completely, nothing to tell there had been a corn field there. Also, on going out to the road and onto the prairie [I saw] all the grass was eaten down into the roots. But the prairie especially was covered with little round holes. Sometimes there would be 100 of them in a square foot. They were also in the garden and all over the yard but thickest on the prairie grass. We dug down in some of the holes [and] they were lined with a sticky substance which would turn water[y] I suppose and filled with grasshopper eggs, ever so many, 100 I think to each hole, so we did not have a very good prospect for the next year. Father said we would have to raise castor beans sunflowers and broom corn which it was supposed grasshoppers would not eat.

So time went on until in November came probably the happiest day of my life when your father came out and joined us. He had stopped in Iowa and tried to get a little rent from the place there and had succeeded in getting a little money on it on a mortgage and he had a little saved from his summer's work probably between 3 and 4 hundred dollars in all. But little we cared then for money or anything it could buy. We were together again and resolved come weal or woe nothing should ever part us again. We were young [and] full of hope and nothing could daunt us.

In a short time your father found a homestead he could get about 2½ miles north and 1 mile west of father's. It had been kind of covered up by a man who was keeping it hid for a relative but there was no trouble in filing it, no contest needed as there were no papers against it. Father and the boys went up with him and broke sod for a house and got the walls up and then it froze up so they could not get sod for the roof. I suppose we were at father's a month or so. They had been around the country a good deal looking for places and to the land office at Bloomington to file etc. etc.

Your father bought me 2 presents when he came. A large family Bible with place for family records and a revolver which he insisted I must learn to shoot. I practiced some to please him and the boys and they all declared me a remarkably fine shot but I never shot any, only as they stood by. I did not desire to kill anything but thought if Indians came I might shoot in self-preservation. Aunt Hattie insisted on us making her a visit before we started keeping house. She knew better than we did how hard it would be to get away afterwards. Father married his second wife again so he had a housekeeper, and we went over to Aunt Hattie's. I don't think we were there much over a week for about the first of February we moved onto our homestead.

As they could not get sod for the roof Uncle Chester went to Juniata with his team and they got 2 x 4[s] and a few boards for roof and to make doors and 3 window sashes and a few boards extra. Even this made a hole in our funds which we could ill afford as we planned to put every cent we could into young cattle as the surest thing in this country.

Then they hauled a load of straw the 7 miles from Uncle Chester's and put on the roof. Everyone prophesied we would burn the roof over our head with the stove pipe running out through the straw roof but your father said not and as I was sure he knew more than any one else I never had a moment's fear.

Then Uncle Chester let us take his big team of horses he had brought from Wisconsin and we went to Juniata and bought stuff to keep house.

That was a proud and happy day long to be remembered. It was an ideal winter day and we bought a new cook stove No. 7 and that was all the furniture we bought as your father had already taken our packing boxes. We had shipped our goods in from Rockford and made Willie a high chair and a bureau and had got lumber for a table and bedstead and made us some stools for seats sawing the tops from logs at Father's. We bought I remember a ½ gallon jug full of vinegar and a gallon jug full of molasses a sack of flour some sugar tea coffee salt and pepper etc. We had no idea how long they would have to last or I fear we would have gotten a larger supply. We did not forget to get a hoe and rake. But we spent a very happy day planning how soon we could have a horse team and things good as Aunt Hattie, meanwhile not caring for anything so [long as] we were together.

We went to Aunt Hattie's that night and the next morning early Uncle Chester took us to our "home" and went to Father's and got what we had there and brought us and we were moved. And happy, no millionaires in their mansion had anything more in that line than we did in our half finished sod house with a straw roof. We had a few boards put down in one end for a floor just large enough for the stove bedstead table and 3 chairs. We hung the carpet we had bought in Rockford up across then for a partition and by hanging an extra quilt and some sheets around on the sod walls made them seem homelike and put up some pictures and behold we had a home and no rent to pay. Who could ask for more? J.T.'s tool chest had to be in the house in the day and with his trunk and mine we had a lot of seats.

Then the next thing was to buy some cattle before we used up all our money so after some hunting around we got about 16 head I think, steers but 1 part-Jersey heifer, a long yearling, a delicate little thing with big eyes we called Lady. We had saved a little money for a well and got a chance to get a breaking plow and [?] in breaking and Papa traded his fine watch for an old wagon we found was over 30 years old. It was most wore out but we had to have a wagon. It had never been worth as much as the watch but we did not know that or that our neighbors would cheat us. Two things stand out in memory while we were at Father's. We had been bothered some with mice and Aunt Hattie had lent us her old gray mother cat with many charges to be good to her and bring her back as soon as she got the mice all caught. Father had bought a few bushels of corn for his horses and hens and in lack of any better place it was piled on the ground between house and barn. The boys spoke several times about seeing rabbits around it and shot one or two and one night your father stepping out saw one as he supposed. Coming back he quickly took down Fred's gun stepped to the door and bang—killed Aunt Hattie's cat. You can imagine our feeling[s] better than I can describe them.

Another time my father and your father, or as we often called them J.M. and J.T., got to boasting how far they could run barefoot in the snow. Finally they put up some kind of a bet each that they could go the fartherest. Just as they pulled off their boots and socks J.T. whispered to me to hand him a clean pair of woolen socks which I did and he slipped them in his coat pocket. I did not see what he wanted of them but the boys and

I were all excited to see the race. Well they ran quite a distance out in the soft snow. Finally my father J.M. started [to tire] and ran back. J.T. went a few steps more and came back and then he showed the socks and said he had them in reserve to come back in if he got very cold and J.M. got ½ sore and said if he had some in his pocket he would have gone farther so they called it a draw.

While we were at Aunt Hattie's she made out a list of garden seeds to send to James Vick and she helped me to select what I needed and we sent together. She gave me a lot of good advice about varieties, always to get the staple ones and then perhaps one or 2 new ones to experiment with and for pleasure. But for this I might more easily [have] been misled by the glowing accounts of new varieties. She told of some of her amusing experiences and gave a lot of good advice as to the difference of soil and climate between here and back in Wisconsin. She had been home to Wisconsin on a visit the fall before and brought some seeds with her and had some of her own raising which she divided with me. So long before planting time I was as eager to get the seeds in the ground as if no such thing as grasshopper eggs abounded.

We had such a nice open winter until after we brought the cattle home. We thought spring was near at hand. They had only a straw stack for food and shelter where they were and we planned on their eating the buffalo grass which was all round our place where it had grown fast after the grasshoppers left. And [there was] a small corn stalk field near to help out. But one night we heard the wind begin to howl in a cold piercing note and J.T. got up to see what was going on. He reported a regular blizzard was starting and we must try to get the cattle in the house or they would drift away and perhaps freeze to death. I hurried to dress and he made me put on his overcoat as he said the wind would blow right through me and I went out into the storm to help him. We opened the south door and drove them to the south side of the house and by considerable running and shouting urged them into the house, all but one stubborn steer. We had him to the door time and again but he always bolted by so as the storm was increasing and we were nearly frozen ourselves we left him go and went back to bed to get warm. I was afraid our carpet partition would not keep them out of our end of the house but J.T. laid on that side of the bed and when they crowded up against the partition he would hit them and shout so they soon crowded into the other end of the room and let us go to sleep.

The next day the blizzard was still on and as fuel was so scarce J.T. said Willie and I must stay in bed while he rustled a fire and something to eat. So he got a good fire and hot water and coffee. I am quite sure we still had some oatmeal though no milk. Anyway he put a coat around me and I sat up in bed and as the stove was right beside I could reach over and see to things and we had quite a lot of fun out of it. J.T. would dance around to keep warm and sing funny songs and as of course Willie wanted to get up he would take him and toss him a bit near the stove and then tuck him back in bed. He went out to try to get the wild steer in but it only made him run further from the shelter of the house so he gave it up. There was nothing we could do for the cattle in the house so J.T. soon came back to bed as we could not burn up all the fuel trying to warm the house and we put in the day telling stories and singing songs until it was time for the other meal ("only 2 meals when the man cooks") which was about the same as breakfast and then to bed again and listen to the blizzard.

The next morning it was still cold but the sun shone bright so we turned the cattle [out] as the wind had died out and the snow which had seemed to come for a night and a day so fast and furious had nearly all, as J.T. said, blown into gopher holes or down into Kansas, so the cattle could get their feed all right and even the steer who stayed outdoors, as he had sheltered himself in the lee of the doorway, seemed not the worse for the storm.

Most of the winter was mild. Having no well as yet we brought our water from the lagoon across the road south of the house and I remember that most of the time I took the dipper and broke the ice but I suppose in the coldest weather J.T. got the water. However it must have been in February that we tried to break some of the steers to plow but poor work we made of it as we did not understand them any more than they did us, and for many years we laughed at all the crooked furrows we made everywhere and most especially across some land we did not want plowed but the steers went anyway. Finally brother Fred came up with his expert lariat hand and gee hawed or gee whooshed them into order. He was the best hand with a wild steer or cow or horse I ever heard of, never cruel to them either. The wildest cow I ever saw, one no one else had ever touched, we wanted tied up so she would not spook the other cattle. We gave it up and J.T. said we better drive her out and let her go but Fred walked up alongside, shot his long left arm about her neck [and] said "Come along old girl" [and] led her to the manger and tied her up. So with the steers he lined 6 or 8 of them strung out on the plow. J.T. held the plow and Fred drove the steers for a straight furrow and after one furrow was laid it was easy for him, but for us they all wanted to get in the furrow at once.

One morning J.T. said he was going to hook a pair of the new steers onto the wagon and for me to get in and we would go and visit the Strohls. I asked if he thought we could get them to go that way and he said yes, just get them pointed south and he was sure they would keep in the road till we got to the corner near their house [and] then he would turn them.

We had made the first track over that road but the boys and J.T. going and coming had made it quite a little track by now. So I dressed up as much as I could and dressed Willie who could now walk real good and we got in the wagon on our board seat, for we did not get a seat with the wagon or even a board but J.T. put some cleats on the ends of our wagon board so it would not shift endwise which was a great improvement over most of them. J.T. got the steers headed into the track [and] then jumped into the wagon. It of course made a noise and the steers did not know what it was or why it bounded along after them so they began to run faster and faster and finally to gallop but they kept to the road and J.T. said that was all they needed to plow, just have a furrow for each one. When we got a mile south to the corner J.T. jumped out ran ahead of them and turned them east. They turned so sudden, for they were on the gallop, they near turned the wagon over but it righted. J.T. jumped in again and we dashed up to Strohls in great style.

They were quite excited and thought it was a runaway but saw we enjoyed it. But Mrs. Strohl said *nothing* would induce her to ride behind such wild steers. Meeting her in Colorado 49 years after she spoke of our first visit when we dashed up with our wild steers.

We had a good visit and a good dinner and she gave me a lot more garden seeds. I told her I had quite a lot but she said "Always plant too much so you will have enough." Good advice.

We traded Pa a yoke of young steers and some boot for a team of broke oxen. He had 2 teams, a big team of natives Buck and Bright, as large oxen as I ever saw, and a team of Cherokee Indian oxen about 1100 pounds weight, spotted as I think most Cherokee cattle were. I do not remember why but probably because the natives were better broken they mismatched them and we got Bright and Jerry. And a funny team they made, Bright so awful large and so terrible awful slow and Jerry so much smaller and bright and quick. It was as hard for him to keep pace with Bright's slow moves as it was for J.T. to slow himself down to them.

We had a bored well put down 86 feet I think [and] got fine water and lots of it. Had to haul it in a long zinc bucket made to go inside to curl and with a windlass and rope wound around a drum but it was very hard work for me. I could hardly manage to get a bucket up at all and it so exhausted me that J.T. forbade me to try it unless absolutely necessary. It seems strange now to think of all the work I did and yet it was like that, anything to [do] that took much strength I simply gave out.

Father gave me 8 Brahma hens and a rooster after we got settled and their eggs were quite an addition to our living though some of them soon wanted to set and I wanted to raise as many chickens as possible and had never heard of an incubator so saved eggs and set them as fast as I could. We had no cupboard and no money to buy more boards so as spring came on we took up the piece of a floor and J.T. made a cupboard out of it. It takes a lot of boards to make a cupboard, top bottom sides back and front besides the deep shelves. But it is still doing duty. We moved the stove table and cupboard over to the west end, and the east end with the bed and bureau I imagined to be the parlor [and] fixed up some curtains and with nice quilted spread it did look nice. As soon as the ground was fully thawed out we began work in earnest. The ¼ section cornering us on the S.E. was taken as a timber claim and five acres plowed and put into trees mostly cottonwood cuttings. The stand was not very good as they had had corn among it and it had not been cultivated much so the corn had been very short and scattering. John Ellis rented it and as the North part had the most trees on it which would have to be hoed around he let us have that part for our garden if we would tend the trees and I think we gave him something else. But I am sure he got the whole thing for taking care of the trees which we now had to do as there were none on the part he kept. Or if there were a few he plowed them up. They put their garden there as like us they had only sod at home but they did not put in [as] much garden as we did. Put theirs into corn or oats I think. I believe we got him to plow our part and harrow it and I began to put in everything I thought would stand a freeze.

Most everyone said it was too early but I wanted an early garden if possible. J.T. helped me lay it out (on paper first) and we had great fun and interest in just how and where and when to plant everything. I suppose we nearly wore the poor seeds out handling them over and over wondering how far they would go etc. We brought some dirt over from the field and put in boxes in the window for tomato and cabbage and sure we enjoyed life those days in spite of not much to eat. But just as most the eatables gave out our heifer got a little heifer calf. She was so small and dainty it did not seem she could give much milk but she gave quite a bit and it was very rich and Willie could have bread and milk to drink and we had milk gravy as well as mush and milk so we used most of it. But once in a while I would save a night's and morning's milk for butter and let it sour and then we would get a good pound of butter and have the sour milk for cottage cheese. Of course it did not make but a little but it made one meal go down good for by now we were nearly out of wheat flour and had got a grain sack full of shorts from the mill and some corn meal as it was cheaper than flour, but though it is good once in a while we missed our good wheat bread and could hardly eat the other.

We had potatoes but not much to go with it and for a couple of months there was just a little sugar in the bowl. No tea or coffee only a little saved for company but we did not miss that so much. But shorts bread and potatoes are not much to work on and we both got poor and weak. But Willie seemed to get along all right and indeed he got so much of the milk it helped him out. We did not think we could get trusted at the store and were too proud to ask so got along. J.T. got about 20 acres broke and planted to broom corn.

We let Pa take the steers for Fred to break with and they traded around with the work some way so Pa planted the broom corn I think. The end of his breaking came up near the house and Willie and I tagged him down the furrows a good deal, sometimes about twice a day going clear around. As the furrows were $\frac{1}{2}$ mile long this made us a mile walk but Willie rode on the plow mostly though sometimes his Pa would carry him for now with old Bright and Jerry the plow stayed in good and most to do was walk along. For there was not much to cook and nothing to sew and only one room to sweep sprinkle and sweep for it was a dirt floor so [there] was no scrubbing. So unless at work over in the garden we always met him at the end of the land and was with him at whatever he did. I suppose a hundred times in later years he has said "I wish we were poor again so you would have time to tag me around like you used." But it worried me to see his cheeks getting hollow and his step not so quick and springy as it used to be.

Being on a farm we wanted to get started in everything that could be raised on a farm as soon as possible. We would sit and build castles in the air of how we would get this and that. Oh the farm of our dreams was fair to behold and gave a good living and would enable us to bring up a large family in plenty. That was all we asked of life. To get this we were willing nay anxious to work all in our power. And always we planned for a large family. When Aunt Sophy asked me how many children I was going to have I told her "As many as I can." And J.T. was of the same mind. We both thought as I know now that small families were more often a curse than a blessing. Very seldom one comes from a small family who amounts to much and the world is usually worse off for their being, and so selfishly are they raised no one can live happily with them. So we thought 12 the least number that would do us and 15 would be better. In all our plans we had at least 12.

Well we knew of course one of the first things to do was to raise our own meat and we must get started in hogs. John Ellis had an old chicken-eating razor back sow he had brought from Illinois and she pestered me to distraction by coming up and catching my chickens. She would come on a lope as far as I could see her and spite of all I could do to head her off would run around and around the house till [she] tired out when I would chase her home. She seemed fairly crazy to catch chickens. Well she had a litter of pigs and John sold one to J.T. for $2.00 as soon as it was two weeks old. I did not like the breed [and] feared it would be like its mother but J.T. said he did not know where we could get another and it would probably be all right if we did not let it get a taste of chicken. But no sir, no sooner had it come than it began to chase chickens and it kept me busy watching it. It was rather a cute little pig for that and we gave it a good deal of our milk but nothing would satisfy it but to smell chickens and run after them and in spite of me it got one occasionally. We had no pen for it and nothing to make one of but shut it in a little box at night. It soon became the pest of my life and when we had had it about 4 weeks I went to the garden one day. At such times I would get Willie to play with it or shut it in the box but this time I was coming right back so put it and Willie in the house. Some way I felt very uneasy and ran back as fast as I could and on opening the door got an awful shock. There lay Willie flat on his back, the pig standing on his chest with its snout in his mouth and the blood running freely down both sides of Willie's face. He could not make a noise as his mouth was full of pig's snout. Of course I grabbed the pig but it was fairly crazed to get back for more blood but I finally threw it out the door.

Willie had found his voice by that time and was so covered with blood it took some time washing him to see how bad he was hurt. Finally found big gashes inside of his lip and in his tongue on the underside mostly. I was terribly frightened but there was no one near so after a while it stopped bleeding and while he had a very sore mouth for some time no great harm was done.

Father came up in a day or so and he was disgusted and

terribly hurt to see his grandson in such a fix. He took the pig home with him and traded us a nice quiet little one for it. He turned his in a large sod pasture with several more but it would run around and squealed for chickens and finally got to climbing the fence and getting them. Then he traded it to Uncle Chester who said he had a tall pen [that] would hold him and it did but it would not [get] fat. It would see chickens cross the yard and stand and squeal after them when its trough was full of milk and corn.

This spring an election was held (I suppose by petition from Hastings people) to try to move the County Seat from Juniata to Hastings. Juniata was much nearer the center of the county and was filled with a better class of business people as Hastings was located by the R.R. interest and was filled with boomers and swindlers of all kinds. Rotten horse traders who shipped old worthless horses they picked up for almost nothing to this country where work horses were greatly needed and sold them at fabulous prices as in the prime of life, sound etc. etc. while I doubt if they ever shipped a reasonable sound animal in.

But if anyone needed money to buy seed or grains or anything which was needed to farm with the town was full of money lenders the most of whom took 10 times the needful security and as a great favor procured your money "from a friend in the east" at never less than 2 come 10 and I have known the Updike Brothers to charge 7 come 10 interest. Three per cent come was the usual charge if you were not too hard up and it meant that to borrow a hundred dollars for seed or harvest hands or anything you gave a mortgage on everything you had and all your future prospects for $100 at 10% interest. Then if it was to run 6 months 3% a month or $18 was kept back. The note was made for 100 and 10% interest but you only got 82 dollars. This was the business that started a number of soon wealthy families and they were known as 3 come 10ers. At the time the Updikes tried to charge us 7 come 10 they assured us there was more demand for their money at that rate than they could supply. As this was needed to farm with and in the spring we could have afforded to pay any reasonable interest but for 6 months we would only have received 58 dollars and given note for 100 and 10% interest, no wonder the Updikes soon became millionaires and great ones on the Chicago board of trade.

Then if you had to go there and hauled your wheat there you likely had to take 2 cents a bushel less than Jim Sewell would have given you at Juniata as they seemed to figure you were there and had to sell but I have known of more than 1 load being hauled back to Juniata. So when it came to vote for the County Seat all the western and southern part of the county went and voted for Juniata. That was J.T.'s first vote and he felt quite set up over it. But a short time after a man drove up in an open buggy to the house door and as J.T. happened to be in he went to the door. He soon came back in and with a curious smile so as not to scare me said "I am arrested and the sheriff is going to take me to Juniata to stand trial for illegal voting." To tell the truth he had not cared to vote being a Canadian by birth. He had declared his intentions to [become] a U.S. citizen on filing papers for our homestead but this must have been in April I think and he had not been in Nebraska 6 months. However Father and all the neighbors that we thought knew assured him it was all right as I had been here longer and we thought they knew. Well that was a long anxious day for me [with] no one to talk to and no idea as to whether he would be found guilty or not. I knew we had no money to pay a lawyer and that he would have to go without his dinner unless the sheriff fed him. But about dark he came walking home.

Juniata had furnished a lawyer to defend him and he had proved that as his wife and baby and all his household goods had been here nearly a year his home was where they were. And that every man was entitled to a home and he had no other except where his family was. So he had stayed and heard a number of other cases some before and others after his and often referred to them.

One case was that of a young man whose parents lived in Kearney County and it was claimed he was not 21 years of age and that his home was with his parents. He had worked for O.H. Wright a year or two and was large and old enough looking for over 21.

The Hastings people had brought his old mother into court to swear to his age but when she was sworn her lawyer told her "If you have no written record of this young man's age, the law allows you 2 years for [lack] of memory." "Well" she said "then

I believe he is 21." So that settled that. In short Hastings lost out badly but they were not satisfied. One night a lot of masked and armed men went up to Juniata and seized all the books and records belonging to the county and moved them to Hastings. I believe Juniata tried some kind of legal proceedings which were put off until Hastings was so boomed that another vote, especially with them to count the ballots, was useless.

Willie did not have any boughten toys but his father always when in the house was whittling something which usually turned out to be something for Willie so he had quite a collection of things including a little wagon about 6 inches long to pull with a string. Then J.T. got hold of some wood and put in a long while making him a larger wagon for out of doors. He had quite a time a[t] Father's and all around to find wood suitable for wheels and tongue etc. But at last it was finished and we were all proud of it. It promised to be useful as well as a plaything but alas we only had it a few days and it was close to the house when some men called Halloo and when I went out they wanted to know the way to some farmer's and as I told them they turned. One said "Look out for the little boy's wagon" but the other laughed and drove directly over it completely demolishing it. They had no business so close to the house but city folks were too lazy to get out and knock.

While I was at work in the garden one afternoon Mrs. Powers an oldish lady who lived 2 miles south surprised me by walking up to see me. She came over to the garden and of all the discouraging things she said first I had too much of it, enough for half a dozen families, next it was too early [and] she had not thought of making [a] garden yet and then you know the hoppers would soon hatch out and I would not have a thing anyway etc, etc. We went over to the house. I felt shy about taking her in the sod house as I knew they had moved a frame one from Lancaster County where they had farmed and Mr. Powers had told everybody they did not like sod houses and that they shipped flour and lard and meat enough to do them a year. So I was greatly surprised when she began to tell how hard up they were. She asked if I had any flour [and] I said "Yes just a little I am saving for company." She said she had about a quart she had to use along to make gravy and did not know when they could get more. We got to telling what we had and did not have and I mentioned having a little molasses left. She asked if I had any ginger and I had some I had brought from Rockford. "Why" she said "you could make a ginger cake. Say, if you will make one I will stay to supper." I dreaded to have her stay as there would not be much to go with the ginger cake but finally considered my company I had saved for was there and to make the best of it.

So we went out and raked around for old stalks and little willow sticks and some "cow chips" to make a fire. She said she was in a hurry to get home before dark so for me to go to making the cake right away and she would make the fire. She thought my little stove too small for any use. She had a number 9 and it was not big enough. I cautioned her not to make much fire as the oven heat[ed] so quick and molasses burns quick but she kept saying it did not hold half the fuel hers did and it was hard to get hers hot. I told her and told her but as I fixed potatoes and thought [that] while I was doing I would do all I could [and] made some hot bread with part flour and [was] setting the table, first I knew the cake was burning. Oh my it was black outside and dough inside and the oven still heating so we had to leave both oven doors open to finish it.

I called J.T. for early supper and it was quite a feast for us and we enjoyed the meal as much or more than she did. I remember I started to scrape off the burnt cake which was really black outside but she stopped me [with] "Oh my don't waste a bit of it. It is all good." In a month or so she had her last baby, being then over 50 years old but the little thing did not see many months.

J.T. kept breaking and one day I remember old Bright stopped in the furrow holding up one foot. J.T. hit him with the whip and hollered to him to go on but he did not stir so he walked around to the side to see if anything was the matter and there lay Willie fast asleep in the furrow and if Bright had set his foot down he would [have] had to set it right on him. Needless to say J.T. got a lesson not to force a reluctant team to go unless you know whether there is a reason why they do not wish to.

The garden began to come up in April and as we had perfectly lovely weather things started to grow very fast and every morning I ran literally ran I was so eager to see how much things had grown over night and then nearly the first of May the hoppers hatched. Yes hatched i[n] millions and billions. One of the neighbors who had out a little small grain came one day and said "Well nothing can live over two days. The hoppers will have every green thing eaten."

And then that night came a blizzard from the north and first came sleet or rain that froze ice over everything it touched and later turned to snow with [the] hard north wind. We had very little fuel and that little was wet. We managed a little breakfast some way but I was so chilled and everything so wet the roof leaking so badly J.T. insisted on my putting on his overcoat while he put on one his brother Donald had left us which was large and he could put Willie inside and going to neighbor Ellis[es] till the storm let up. They had a dugout and shingled roof so we knew they would be comfortable especially as he had a team of mules so had been able to haul wood. It was ¾ of a mile west and I did not believe I could make it and would rather go to bed but there was no dry place for the bed and J.T. rolled the bedding up as small as he could to keep it dry. You see before this we had taken the straw roof off and put on a sod roof but the rafters were so light we could not put much dirt on so it leaked and leaked, muddy water at that. Well J.T. got me on the south side of him and Willie in his coat but some way I could hardly walk and he had to help me along with his arm around me and then just as we got to the door and the warm air struck me I fainted and nearly fell.

When I recovered I found myself in bed with warm irons to my feet but I did not feel very well all day so do not think I got up. Nor did I seem to want to eat or drink, just to lie still in a kind of stupor. J.T. went back home to see to the stock and about getting some kind of fuel raked up [and] probably went over to the garden for small pieces of old corn stalks and put [them] in the house.

But the next morning the sun was shining bright and it soon got nice and warm, the wind having gone down, and we went home and took things out in the sun to dry. But the hoppers were every one dead. And I have never seen any more of that kind of hopper to this day. I notice some writers give 1875 as the last visit of the hoppers around here and it is easily explained. For they were travelling like a large cloud and many places for miles they did not light and we found that not many miles away they had not lit and so they might easily not know that they were around as we did not travel much those days and had no phones to spread the news. I know we were surprised when we found that it was not far to the edge of the hopper territory but we did not find it out for a long time.

As soon as we got the broom corn planted J.T. said he thought we had stood enough and he was going out to look for some work to get some victuals. So one morning he started to walk to Hastings where we heard there was some building going on and I went to work in the garden for by now I could put in the later things. I was still working in the garden and the sun was about an hour from setting when here he came walking back. He had been to Juniata and all over Hastings to anyone or any place it looked there might be work [and] then got a ride part way to Kenesaw and looked around there and then walked home. Must have walked over 40 miles but no sign of work. Then we heard of someone down by the Blue [who] wanted 20 acres' breaking done so J.T. took the oxen and went down there. Slow as they were it would take about a day to go but he took Willie and I down to Father's to stay while he was gone. I did not like to leave my hens and young chickens but was afraid to stay alone. So the next morning brother John got on a horse and went up to milk the cow and see to the chickens. He came back and said something had killed several chickens so they took me home right away and sister Susie went with me for company. That afternoon we were all quiet in the house and I heard a hen make a little scared noise and looking out the north door saw what I supposed was a little dog which I thought must have got lost from a mover's wagon. So I called Willie to see the little dog as I thought he would like it for a pet but it ran around the house and I opened the south door and called come doggie doggie and there it came with a chicken in its mouth and then I saw it had bushy tail so I took the broom and chased after it and it dropped the chicken and ran way very swift. I never saw another animal like it but folks told me it was a Swift, a kind of prairie fox smaller than a coyote.

The days went pretty slow without J.T. How I wished there was something to read and sometimes I wished I did not know how to read so I would not want to, as I noticed people who did not know how seemed to get along quite contented. But there were months when we did not see a paper and the few books we had I almost knew by heart. One day we found John Ellis was going to town and I gave him the last money we had 15 cents to get a half bushel of whole corn. I needed some for the chickens but could not think of anything else to eat so good for the money. I would not have been so extravagant if I had not thought J.T. would soon be back with $40 for the breaking. It seems now that was one of the longest days of my life. We went over to the garden and found some little pieces of corn stalks and brought [them] home so we could make a fire quick when we saw him coming. Probably hunted up some dry cow chips too if there were any around.

At last here he [John Ellis?] came and he had about ½ bushel of shelled corn. My but it looked good. We got a fire going soon as we could and parched a skillet full for our supper, the best meal for a long time. I think J.T. must have been gone nearly 2 weeks for the oxen were very slow but he crowded them all they would stand as he wanted to get home and do some more breaking for ourselves and raise some sod corn.

Finally he came and as soon as I saw him I knew something terrible had happened he looked so woe be gone.

Well to make it short everything went all right till he got the breaking done and was ready to start home. Then the man said "I have no money now but will pay you next fall." J.T. was thunderstruck. He had never heard of such a rascal. He said he felt like taking 40 dollars' worth out of his hide but did not but came home and then we were worse off than before and we might have had so much more breaking done for ourselves. Really I do not believe we ever got a cent from the fellow and I am not sure whether J.T. ever went to see about it. We put it down a[s] work stolen by a dishonest man and let it go I think for of course the fellow never intended to pay it in the first place.

So he started breaking for sod corn on our own place and I dropped the corn every third furrow. By dropping it right on the edge it came up through the crack between two furrows and sometimes made quite a little corn and even if it only made fodder it would help out. I think we planted some of my ½ bushel but I know Father gave us some white flint corn Grandpa Sanford sent from Wisconsin, the same kind salesmen sell now as the Sanford corn, and also gave us some dark blue or purple squaw corn which was supposed to be somewhat grasshopper proof for we thought the hoppers might come again that fall. So I would go around dropping 3 kernels about 3 feet apart and to get them on the edge was slow work so it took quite a while to drop it. We soon found a little gopher was taking up a lot of the corn on the end nearest the house.

That would never do so J. T. set a trap in the furrow and we went on and when we came back behold we had one of the Brahma hens by the neck and she was *dead*. I expect I shed a few tears but she was fine eating which helped some.

Later he did some breaking for T. B. Burns. He did not get any money but whatever he was to get he got but I forget now what it was, a stirring plow or harrow or what but I know it was not money.

By now the early radishes were being used and they were good and we were glad there was so many of them, also of the lettuce and young onions. If we could have had bread with them we would not have asked for more but the shorts did not go so well, however they helped out a lot. It must have been toward the last of June he was breaking for Burns and he would leave the oxen to feed on the grass there and walk back and forth and nearly 3 miles by the road but something over 2 crosslots. His boots were so near wore out he had to save them and go barefoot and as he had not done so since a boy his feet got very sore walking over the prairie. It is fun to go barefoot in the furrow but on the prairie there were lot[s] of stubs of burnt shoestring (a low shrublike plant).

One day while he was breaking there the oxen gave a snort and jumped clear out of the furrow and as he was not expecting anything of the kind but tightened his hands on the plow handles it gave him a big jerk, and looking down he saw the furrow full of pieces of rattlesnake which had evidently been coiled in the furrow and the short rolling cutter had cut into several pieces. These were threshing around and the head with mouth open trying to bite. Needless to say he was not long getting out of that furrow. He would not get home until after dark but we were having lovely moonlight nights.

As we had no kerosene nor fat enough to make a light with a rag as many did (what they called a slut) I would get the table set out by the south door where the light would strike it and gather old corn stalks and old grass, anything that would make a light fire. Then having set the table with such green stuff as I could gather from the garden as soon as he came I would light the fire and make the shorts [into] pancake and we would sit in the moonlight and eat our supper. One night while so eating and talking and laughing my father came up on horseback. He came to the back door and called Hulloo [to] the house, have you gone to bed already. J.T. called to him to come around to the south door and he sure was surprised to see us eating our supper by moonlight. And [he] asked where is your light and what the Dickens were you laughing so about. We told him we had no light and whatever it was that had made us laugh, probably something Willie had said or done. But he could not see the fun for once but asked "How long has this been going on, no light?"

"Why" we told him "a month or two."

"And what in the world if you should be sick in the night?"

"Oh we never get sick. We are all right" we told him. But life did not look as gay to him that night as usual and he soon went away and the next morning sent brother John up with a bottle of kerosene with which we filled the lamp and kept it for emergencies.

After supper we would sit on the doorstep in the moonlight. I would have my head on his shoulder with his arm around me and Willie likely on his lap. We would be very tired for we never worked less than 18 hours a day, but even so he used to say he thought he was the happiest man in the world with his family all in his arms and indeed I would not have changed places with anyone on earth. Sitting now in the sunset glow of life I realize that those summer evenings were the best of life. We had youth, love, and hope. What more could anyone want?

One day when coming from the garden with a bunch of

radishes in my hands a man driving by the road asked what I would take for them. I did not know him but knew by his looks he did not have a surplus of money so I said two cents. "All right" he said and passed over 2 pennies and I went back and got us some more. But right way after that I read a letter from Aunt Lizzie and she said the grandchildren were giving 10 cents each to get Grandma Smith a birthday present and she thought I would want to contribute. Want to, I felt that no one except J.T. and the baby were so dear to me as her, my dead mother's mother who had always been so dear to me. And I only had 2 cents and it took 3 to get a postage stamp. I might have gotten a postal card I suppose but no one was going to town for a month or so while I could have sent a letter by someone passing. So I could not even write and say I would have [been] delighted to send if in my power and I shed quite a few bitter tears in secret for I would not let J.T. know how much I cared and make him unhappy for he could not help it.

Along in the summer it got very dry. No rain for a long while. Every night a cloud would come up in the southwest and we would anxiously watch for rain and sometimes it came close enough so we could smell it but never a drop came our way. The garden looked so wilted [that] every night I would think it could not stand another day but in the morning it would look quite fresh again. Finally one night I had J.T. go over to the garden with me to see how long he thought things could live and the same cloud came up in the southwest and as I looked at it I said "Oh if it would only rain I would not care if I got wet to the skin." For the roof leaked so whenever I said I wished it would rain he would ask if I wanted to get wet. And we dared not put on more dirt to stop it leaking as some of the rafters had cracked as it was. So we laughed and he teased me a little and said probably I would if I got my wish and we went home and to bed as it seemed to have gone around. After a little the most terrible thunder and lightning woke us up and it began to rain in torrents. This was a little before John had brought the kerosene. No sooner did the rain strike the roof than it struck the bed. "Here we must get up and roll up the bed" said J.T. "and probably we can find a place large enough to stand in." No sooner said than we were out. He took Willie in his arms and rolled the bed up in a second so the bottom side was up and as small as he could and I ran around to try to find a dry place in the dark but I could not find one but succeeded in getting wet to the skin all right and my nightgown was not only wet but muddy.

J.T. however was more fortunate and called me to come close to him and we would be all right. So there we stood while the rain seemed to come down to buckets full which was the way when a long drouth would be broken and we stood and laughed. Laughed because I got my wish. Laughed because it was so ridiculously funny. I laughed for joy for my garden. J.T. laughed because of it all and because I did. We would nearly stop and Willie would begin and then we would begin all over again. Finally even laughing could not keep my teeth from chattering in my wet gown but right away then the rain stopped. J.T. unrolled the bed which was warm and dry on the inside and "sweet we cuddled down" again [and] soon got warm and dry.

The next morning, as always after those showers, the sun was gloriously warm and bright. The garden was fine as possible but I had a job housecleaning and washing and drying our clothing but was glad that it was necessary just so we got the rain. We had many a good laugh over our wetting for years to come and I don't think I ever said I wished it would rain that J.T. did not ask if I was willing to be wet to the skin.

Meanwhile we were doing real well with our chickens. I would give the chickens from 2 or 3 hatches to one hen and set the others over. We had to save most of the eggs to set to do this as we only had 7 hens now. As we had very little feed I would drive them off east of the house to a knoll of buffalo grass when the seed had ripened very early and they throve well on it with a little bran at night. But of course they were not ready to eat as soon as if they had had more feed. We began to eat one once in a while when they were quite small, about harvest time I think, and as they got larger we ate them often in spite of which we had about 90 hens and pullets to keep over for another year. So we were well satisfied.

As everything was spring grain then harvest did not come until late after the middle of July I think and J.T. went to work for O.H. Wright for harvest. O.H. was probably the best off farmer in the county. He had brought a lot of horses, machinery and stock of all kinds from Michigan 2 or 3 years before and now had a large herd of cattle and kept several hired men at times. He was unable to do very much himself owing to a wound got in the civil war but did a good deal of business riding and had the first and only riding tools around for a long time.

It was always customary and understood that harvest wages were not due nor to be paid until after threshing. Still it was something to have something coming sometime. It was about $3\frac{1}{2}$ miles to go to work but we got up early and J.T. always drew enough water from the well for the oxen and cow and house before he went, and as he worked at least 12 hours pitching bundles or stacking or binding bundles by hand he must have gotten very tired. But he never complained. I would usually be in bed before he came as it would be long after dark but I would hear him whistling a long way off and often get up and run to meet him.

During this time we had been having peas and beans from the garden young carrots and beets and beet greens and a lot of things but nothing seemed to take the place of bread. We did not say anything about it but I was so ornery. It seemed the more I had the more I wanted bread and nothing would take its place. Night after night and nights without number I dreamt of bread. Mostly seemed as if I was at Grandpa Sanford's big table loaded with everything as it always was and big stacks of bread as there always was and good big slices and plates of Grandma's golden butter. Sometimes the bread was passed and I actually had it in my hands and wondered if this was a dream and thought no this time it is real. But always something happened and I woke up before I got to taste it and many times I cried a little softly to not let J.T. know because I had to wake up. It did seem too hard not to be able even to eat it in my sleep.

But when Saturday night came after J.T. went to work for O.H. (for all the country called him O.H. instead of Wright just as they called Father J.M. and Uncle Chester C.C.) when I went to meet J.T. he had a heavy load probably 50 pounds of flour he had carried home. I think good Aunt Pauline, as everyone called Mrs. Wright who was a mother to everyone and every colt calf pig chicken and living thing on the place, had probably found out by asking J. T. questions that we had no flour and as they had taken wheat to mill he brought this home.

Willie was asleep when he came home and would not have known the difference in flour anyway but the next morning for breakfast we had hot biscuits and as I placed them on the table Willie's eyes grew big and bigger. He pointed a little finger at them and said "That's boo ah" which seemed to mean it was the real thing no imitation. We did not know he had missed the bread for he was a happy hearty little fellow but the way he ate proved that he liked the real thing as well as we did and we both laughed and cried to see him eat. I set some light bread right away and that was the end of those hard times. By now the tomatoes were so we could use them and cucumbers and musk-melons and sweet corn [and] the watermelons of which I had bought the earliest varieties. Seemed too many of them stopped growing but neither of us knew how to tell when they were ripe. I wished for Pa or one of the boys to come and tell us but they were busy and we were afraid to waste one by cutting it too green so we let them be.

One day I was over in the garden in the sweet corn which was near the watermelons when I heard a man jump off a wagon going by the road while the team went slowly on. He ran into the melon patch and picked one up. Then seeing me he let it slide down to his feet and came toward me saying "I saw you over here and thought I would see if I could buy a melon."

"Why" I said "I guess you could but I don't know as any are ripe so we have not eaten any yet."

He thumped one. "This is ripe" he said. "What will you take for it?"

"A nickle" I said and he gave it to me quickly and ran to catch his team. I then went to where he dropped the one and carried it home and as soon as J. T. came in we cut it and it was fine and ripe. First we thumped it to see how it sounded so we could tell the rest. And we found we had a lot of ripe melons so had all we wanted all fall and besides I had 7 cents now.

We planned to put up a whole lot of hay because there was an endless lot no one else would use and we had quite a little stock and especially we planned to sell hay to the freighters and movers going by. For we were on the freight road between the western valleys and Juniata and Hastings. And as there was no railroad in all that section nearer than the Union Pacific all wheat and things to sell were freighted from all the S.W. part of the state and N.W. Kansas past us and all kinds of groceries and dry goods for stores were hauled back. Men made a winter's job of it and most of the return stuff was shipped to Hastings so they went there but if they did not have a return load they usually stopped at Juniata. There was a long stretch between Beal's ranch and any ranch west and we rightly judged that if we had a lot of hay and room in the barn for a couple of extra teams we could get a little money through the winter. So to get ready to put up the hay at which I planned to help we got home a yoke of the steers which were so much spryer than the oxen and were now pretty well broken, and J.T. went down on sand creek or somewhere south for a load of brush so I could get the meals quicker. I went with him as far as Father's and spent the day there for I had not been there for so long.

It was real dark before J.T. got back and of course they had him come in and eat and wanted us to stay all night as Father did not think it safe for us on that high load of brush when we could not see the road. And across the big Griswold hill where there was no bridge and another little creek which had steep banks it would be easy to upset. In fact we would be sure to if a few inches out of the road. But J.T. said it would be all right so I knew it would be and we went. The steers were anxious to get home and as the load mostly willows was more bulky than heavy they travelled at a good pace. In fact going down the hill by Griswold's and the other little pitches they ran and jumped across the bottom which seemed fun to us as we knew then where we were. Of course there were no lines on the steers so as I did not want J.T. blundering along by their side and he thought it would be unnecessary he rode, and we laughed and sang and Willie went to sleep and finally I dozed off a little before we got home. I would not take that ride again for anything but it was great fun then and we often spoke of it in later years.

I think brother Fred came up with their horse team on the mower and J.T. traded work with them some way. He raked after the mower and having cut down as much as we wanted to handle at once Fred went home and we started to put up our hay. Willie would stay on the ground with his Pa and I would load and then we would take the load home, sometimes a mile or two, as we cut mostly the draws and I would stack while J.T. pitched it off.

It was while coming home with a load that Willie said his name for the first time. We were all sitting on the load and playing. We would throw a little hay over Willie and then pretend he was lost and say "Where's Willie," and sometimes we would call 2 or 3 times and then he would jump up laughing but soon he would lie down again to be covered up. It was getting a little old at last for us and after we covered him up we spoke of something else and forgot him. He lay still quite a bit for him and then he called out "Where's Willie?" That sure pleased and surprised us. J.T. grabbed him and hugged him and said "You blessed little Scotchman. Where did you get the burr on your tongue?" And it did seem strange he should speak broad Scotch when he never heard anyone. This pleased J.T. greatly for though he was always telling jokes on the Scotch he was very proud of his Scotch blood. Much as I enjoyed helping with the hay which was so clean and smelt so sweet I loved to work with it, yet every night I would be so full of pain I could not sleep and it worried J.T. so he got brother Fred to come and stay with us for some time and help us out, for we now planned to take the house for a barn and build a new one with heavy log roof so it would not leak. With that in view the hay was stacked close to the house to be handy to feed the next winter.

Meanwhile I realized I must make over some of my clothes I had before marriage, nice white skirts etc., into baby clothes as there was no prospect of getting anything new but I had no white thread. I had never bought any thread since coming west as there was so little to sew and I had brought some. We paid 5 cents a spool in Rockford and I thought it would be probably 6 here but as a neighbor was going to town I gave him my 7 cents to get a spool of white thread. Imagine my disappointment when he returned me the money and said he could not get the thread as it was 10 cents. So I started sewing the nice white goods by hand with black thread. Jennie (Father's wife) came up with him soon after and was greatly shocked and said she would trade some white thread for black and sent some up and part of the sewing I took out and part I let stay for remembrance because I thought best to do the rest of the sewing first. They put up a large stack of hay beginning at the N.W. of the house running west 50 or 60 feet maybe more in North of the well, the object being to leave this stack till the last of the feed and it would make a good wind break for stock west of the barn and around the well. They got that stack completed and a neighbor came in the morning to borrow the forks and as they were going to mow and rake more hay that day they lent them to him. At noon there was a high wind blowing from the south so they could not have hauled hay but could cut. They came to dinner which was not quite ready as they were a little early. One thing J.T. never had any patience for was a late meal. He justly said it did not take any longer to get it one time than another. I hurried the fire by putting in some of the willow brush. In the strong wind with a straight pipe and no damper in it the blaze ran right up the pipe and a blazing leaf fell onto the end of the stack of hay. J.T. saw it and quick as a cat had grabbed a broomstick and was [on] top of the stack pitching the fire off and Fred was close behind him, but alas while if they had had a fork one fork full would have pitched it all off they could not control it without and in a few minutes all that fine hay was a mass of black ashes. Lesson No. 2 on lending. Lesson 1 was in the spring we had our heifer calf tied to a rack with straw in it for shelter and the same neighbor came and borrowed the rack and did not return it that night as promised. There came a chill rain and wind in the night. The calf chilled and in spite of all we could do died. As it would not have cost us anything hardly to have raised it it was a big loss to us. But J.T. never could or never did refuse to lend anyone anything though many times they could afford them better than we could.

I felt dreadfully about the hay feeling it was somewhat my fault but they would not hear [of] it. They both were there and saw me put the wood in but a stronger gust than usual seemed to whip it around to the N.W. instead of straight North. Anyway it was all to do over again and would be further to haul this time as we had cut around home first. Well they went to work at it after dinner while I watched the ashes which they had wet down some for fear sparks got away and burnt off our grass we wanted for feed.

All this time the broom corn on our sod had been growing and was now 6 or 8 feet tall and about ready to cut but the corn on the sod had not amounted to anything just a stalk here and there with very few nubbins.

By the time they got the hay up again though [it was] not so much nor quite as nice and green as the other. It was time to begin on the broom corn though Fred and J.T. had laid up some of the walls for the new house and hauled some logs and brush for the roof. We tried to get someone to help cut the broom corn, as to have it a nice green color it needs to be cut before frost when it brings best price.

But Fred was needed at home now and we did not know of anyone. I think O.H. must have paid us some or got us some groceries for we now had sugar and coffee and lard and some such things we had to have to have and keep a hired man. So I started in to help J.T. cut the broom corn but we only worked 2 or 3 days when I got sick in the night.

J.T. made a hurried run a mile east for a neighbor woman who hurried back and about daylight we had another lovely little baby boy whom we named at once after his father. I wanted to call the first one James but the family tradition of the Kellies was to have the first son William and the second son James. This was Friday morning September eighth and J.T. stayed around a good deal that day to see if we needed anything etc. but worked a good deal too.

Saturday my father having heard the news he and Jennie came up and she cooked and washed and tended to things generally. Everyone said we had the most beautiful baby they ever saw except Father who said he looked just like their Frankie who died. Saturday night it rained. J.T. fixed a canopy over the bed to keep the rain off from a quilt I suppose but Willie who slept at my feet got wet without my knowing it. Whether it was that or not he took quite a bad cold which made him very feverish and he did not want anyone to touch him but me. Very unusual as he was always well and good natured and liked his Pa and Grandpa better than me I thought. I toused around with him a good deal Sunday and Monday concluded it was easier to sit up and look after him as we were quite worried about him. The new baby was fine and good as pie but being up I got dinner and then being so worried about the broom corn went out and helped cut some. J.T. did not think this just the right thing but what he did not know about sickness or women would make quite a book so he did not stop me and once started I kept on.

Tuesday morning I wrapped the new baby in a quilt and took it to the field and worked all day and did so until I guess Father heard what was going on through some of the neighbors and he drove to Hastings and brought us back a hand Colonel Campbell, a colonel in the civil war on the Southern side. A highly educated man who had been through Harvard and some years' study and travel abroad but they lost their wealth in the war and the love of drink had put him down to the level of a common tramp. Only he never forgot to be gentleman in manner and polite in speech. So then I stayed in the house and got the meals and tended the babies and Willie was soon as well as ever but I did not get real strong for a long time.

J. M. Strohl made a good deal of his living by raising sweet potato plants for sale as he had done in Ohio. He had several large sod beds with cloth covers for them and took a good many plants to Hastings to sell but as he had only an ox team he let Father do most of the selling. They would put the plants up 100 in a bunch and Father paid him $2.00 for 1000 and sold them for $3.00. Then he paid for the plants by doing breaking for Strohl as he [Strohl] devoted most of his time to the plants and gardening, sweet potatoes and onions being their specialty though they raised all kinds of garden in abundance especially melons. We had got a thousand or maybe 2000 plants in the spring and paid in breaking. They had done fine and we began to slip some of them out (without disturbing the hills) quite early in the season to use and enjoyed them immensely.

Now possibly before we began to cut the broom corn but I think we had it cut, J.T. took quite a load of them to Kearney and sold them to a merchant there Harrison by name. He did not like to go to Hastings or Juniata which was nearer as it might interfere with Strohl's market. He had me make out a list of things we would need before we threshed and bailed the broom corn and so well did he do that he got all of them. I think he got some shoes for himself but know he got a pair for Willie for it was getting cool nights and mornings and the shoes he had always had were now too small to get on.

I think Willie was about a week old when his father declared he must have some shoes and went downtown (in Rockford Illinois) and brought home the nicest pair of blue morocco shoes I ever had or have seen for nothing was too good for his boy. He got a pair of No. 1 and they were plenty large but he said he knew he was such a strong hearty boy he would soon grow out of them so he took them back and brought back some No. 3. They were very much too large but he said No. 2 was only a little larger than No. 1 so best be on the safe side and he got 3's.

Of course he did not wear them for a long time as he had little booties but the first summer on cool days and that fall and winter they were just the thing. I took some gray flannel and cut it just like the shoes and piped them with red and had him wear them over the shoes when creeping to save them. In that way and because they were such good stuff when he had outgrown them they looked almost like new.

So now when nearly 2 years old he had his second pair and we had a good supply of groceries which we needed as we would have to have hired help with the broom corn.

Broom corn grows 8 and 10 feet high and is ready to cut when the head comes up out of the boot and must be cut before frost to be first class. A man then goes along and tables it, that is bends the broom corn over two rows together each one across the other. That leaves a flat table and the heads stick out on each side of the table, the heads on row one over on row 2 and the heads on row 2 over row 1. The whole field is bent over that way and the green leaves make it shady under the table and Willie liked to play there and there I put the baby while I worked. They then go along each side of the table and cut off all the heads with a knife like a shoe knife or sharp potato knife. Afterwards the heads are gathered up and put in long ricks to dry and covered with some stalks to keep out wet and the sun from bleaching, as the brighter green and less brittle they are the better the brooms and the higher the price. Then men who owned the machinery would come around with a broom corn thresher and a baler. The heads were held up to the revolving machine by hand and the seeds knocked off which was called threshing and then passed along to the baler. So it called for quite a lot of help and made it cost quite a lot of money for help but they always waited for this money till the broom corn was sold.

The price of broom corn was not near as good as the year before. Still there was something for our work after all.

While the broom corn was drying Fred and J.T. completed one room of our new sod house and took the cupboard he had made from the floor and set it in the wall as part of the partition between the two rooms. They plastered the wall with a light colored clay and later we put in a board floor. This kitchen was only lighted by one south window and the door was in the east. The west had a door going into a large bedroom not finished which was to be bedroom and sitting room and had 2 windows in the south and one in the west. On the north of the kitchen was a door leading down 3 or 4 steps into a large cave for vegetables etc. which would be easily got in the winter. So we were living in this kitchen which was probably 14 x 16 feet when we had the broom corn threshers and balers but the roof was not on the bedroom though the walls were up.

I put up some pictures and we were very comfortable and cozy. As soon as we moved out of the first house J.T. put up posts under the rafters to strengthen the roof and divided it into stalls. And soon he drove the oxen and some of the steers to Hastings and traded them off for a team of dun horses Frank and Bill weighing about 1100 each and 4 and 5 years old. Our good faithful old Standbys.

The end wall of the new house was sod about 2 feet thick and so was the partition wall and a heavy log about a foot thick was laid on top for a center piece. Then long poles also quite large probably 8 or 10 inches at the butt were run from the side walls into the center log.

This was then covered with willow brush and then a layer of sod and a lot of dirt on that and we looked at it in great satisfaction, sure that it would neither break nor leak.

It must have been in November that J.T. was down to Father's for something and the babies and I were alone. I was bending over the washtub washing clothes of which I now had quite a lot to do and which I was never very good at. So it was along in the afternoon and I was still rubbing away on colored clothes. I know now one great trouble was I never used soap enough trying to save soap but then I did not see why other women could get their clothes out early and I had to wash all day. I felt a thrill or quiver or something as if the house shook and looking up distinctly saw the roof move back and forth, the roof I had felt was so secure. I jumped and grabbed the baby and taking hold of Willie we were outside in short time and I fully expected the house would be down on us before we could get out and stood and looked at it expecting every second to see it fall. Everything looked all right. I walked around and looked in at the window for some time. The roof was not moving and everything was all right but it was some time before I ventured back in but finally concluded that I must have been dizzy from bending over the tub so long. When J.T. came home and I told him about it he said it was the same time of day that Jennie being still in bed after George was born had cried out that the bed was shaking and was frightened but none of them that were up noticed anything. After a few days we heard there had been an earthquake felt in some parts of Nebraska at that day and hour so knew that was what it was.

Of course all told it [the house] had taken a lot of work but no money except for the floor and we did not put that in till we had sold the broom corn.

When we had the broom corn sold we did not have very much left after paying for shelling and baling. The price had gone down from the years before so it did not bring near as much as we expected so we put off finishing any of the house but the one room as we had to buy some grain for the horses and had to have some clothes. I took my first trip to town about 18 months after I came and got outing flannel and flannel for underclothes for us all and some things for Willie and also some groceries but we knew we had to go very sparing as it would be a long time till another crop would be ready to sell. But my early pullets were beginning to lay early that fall and kept it up all winter. We had put up a sod coop which was warm and roofed it with straw and there was not a day all winter we did not get some eggs. These I sold mostly to the freighters who were glad to get good fresh eggs at 10 cents a dozen cash and I was equally glad to get the cash.

As our barn would only accommodate 2 or 3 teams we were obliged to send many parties of freighters on but we often had all we could accommodate at 25 cents a team for stable room and hay and the freighter had [a] house room to cook or warm up his "grub" and a place on the floor to spread his quilt. Often the last one to lie down at night took up the last available space. They each carried a "grub box" a common wooden box with cover to keep out snow and containing some bread meat etc. with coffee pot and skillet. Each had one or more quilts which usually were cold and covered with snow either falling or thrown up by the wheels and had to be dried out a little before making down their beds, which was done by spreading down a quilt and folding it back so as to go below and over them. With boots for a pillow and overcoat spread over for extra cover their bed was ready. We piled chairs etc. on top of the table to make as much room as possible and usually when we were full 2 men stuck their feet under the table. Long before light they were up getting their breakfast [and] feeding and harnessing their teams and we would let them get their breakfast first though I always got up as soon as they went out to feed which they always did at once to give me a chance to get up I suppose. When they found I always had good fresh eggs 6 for a nickel they made calculations on getting them. They had often tried to carry them but they usually froze up and were not so nice.

Between the hay and the eggs we had a little spending money this winter but saved it up for seed wheat and corn for the team etc. We enjoyed life on the whole that winter as much as any in our lives. We were so proud of our 2 boys we could hardly contain ourselves and made all kinds of plans for their future. Then with our horse team we were enabled to go to church and went often over into the Chester Clewett and O.H. Wright neighborhood and attended revival meetings there and finally both of us joined the church there. I had belonged to the M.E. Church in Minnesota joining when 14 years of age but your father had never joined any before. He inclined strongly to the foreordination belief of the Presbyterians of which his father was always a leading member but there was no church near and we joined together and it seemed my cup of happiness overflowed.

The preacher was a Reverend Summers a very likable young man with a wife and 2 or 3 young children. She was very pleasant also and besides at the meetings we met them several times visiting at Aunt Hattie's and they came to see us and we became quite attached to them. My father also experienced a revival of his religion that winter and commenced preaching or exhorting again in the Mayflower school house and I think other places.

Your father's lack of religious interest had always been a deep sorrow to me, raised as I had been to think even more of the future life than the present one. I knew my mother and dear friends had gone to Heaven where I hoped to meet them some day and yet I did not want to go there without your father. Without him it would be no Heaven to me so you can see how rejoiced I was and we had Bible reading and prayers at home. And J.T. was sure he would never indulge in a bad temper again and when he got even a little vexed would pray earnestly for forgiveness and strength not to sin again.

Perhaps you wonder how we could go away to church or visiting, especially to evening church while keeping a wayside ranch for freighters but the answer was easy. The latch string always hung out. The house was never locked and the wood box was always kept filled with cut broom corn stalks so a quick fire could be started and when we came home towards night if anyone had been there and fed for dinner we would find a dime for each team probably in a cup on the table.

And usually when we came from evening church the house would be full and warm and the freighters would call out "All full neighbor. Bad luck but you will have to go on to the next place." And often it would look full but they would conclude there could be one more team put in and squeeze in some way. There's always room for one more. So we would go in and some would be cooking and some eating and some would say "Goodness don't let her see those eggs." For they had gathered them and had them cooking. Or "For goodness' sake boys hide that cow," meaning the milk pitcher as they had milked and [were] using a little. But I am sure we never lost a cent by any of them but had many a jolly and happy evening with them.

A funny incident occurred that fall. We were sitting at dinner one Sunday J.T. brother Fred sister Susie Willie and I with baby Jimmie on the bed when a light covered wagon drove into the yard and a young man a cowboy by dress knocked at the door and asked permission to water the team and to know if they could buy a loaf of bread. As I had just baked a good sized batch of bread the day before I got a loaf for which I charged him 5 cents ½ of which I judged to be clear profit and he went out to the wagon. Soon he came back and wanted to know if we would allow them to camp there until the next morning [and] said as it was Sunday they did not care to travel far and could not get to their destination that day anyway without driving very late. Of course we were willing in fact rather enjoyed having company so Fred and Willie went out with him to show him where to camp the wagon and where was good grass to stake out the horses etc.

When he came back he reported they were the jolliest bunch he ever saw just laughing all the time. They had asked him questions and he had told them some about us and they seemed to find something awful funny about us.

The one who came to the door and they called Jim was a cowboy whose parents lived not far east of Hastings and the others cowboy friends [who] were accompanying him for a visit and now when they could have got home that night Jim had got over his hurry and got religious and stopped for the night at noon. J.T. soon went out to get acquainted and invited them into the house and the three came in and seated themselves in a row on the bed for there were not many chairs and no room for chairs either. But they certainly did act queer. One of them would seem to look at me or Willie or the baby and start to say something and laugh and choke and probably have to go outdoors. I got to feeling something must be wrong with us or something [and] looked to see if I had black on my face or something.

Finally I saw J.T. was getting a little riled and I guess they saw it too for one of them spoke up. "Well I guess we have made fools of ourselves long enough [and] we may as well make a clean breast of it and all laugh together. You see when Jim here came back with the bread he said 'Say boys there is a nice girl in there. What say we camp here till morning?' Of course we had thought him in a hurry to get home. He had talked of nothing else for weeks but anything to accommodate him so we unhitched. But when the boy said the girl was the mother of this chap (pointing to Willie) it was just too good to keep. Jim here has been on the range so long he is liable to run off with the first woman he meets."

Well, of course we all laughed together and I know I felt relieved that they were not laughing at me. J.T. told them with emphasis that though they would never find as nice a girl as his they could not have his and we had many good laughs, for once in a while the boys would laugh about what the boys on the range would say to Jim. And how far they ought to be now etc. One of the boys they called Indian Jim. I could not see much difference in looks but he informed us he was $\frac{1}{2}$ French and $\frac{1}{2}$ American [and] said his mother's father was French and his father's mother was a squaw. He sure did not seem to have any Indian stolidity about him that night.

Well they passed out of our lives except Jim who made several trips to and fro to see his folks and so stopped at different times and always told how the boys on the range never forgot that trip but asked him every time he went home if he stopped to see his girl and said they were always interested to hear how we were getting along.

Many of them put in all fall and winter freighting and so made many trips and got to seem like old friends. They were glad to drive in where they were welcome and [found] a good fire and we were glad to see them. In that way we got a good deal of news from the outside world as we as yet took no paper and often some of them left a paper they had got and read.

Brother Fred stayed with us a good deal that winter and went to school and he and J.T. would take ropes into the broom corn field and with a hoe cut the stalks and put them in the rope till they had as large a bundle as they could carry. Then [they would] pull it up tight and bring it to the house [and] then with their knives they would cut it into pieces stove length and fill the big wood box J.T. had built in behind the stove. It took one putting in a good deal in fact almost constantly but by doing so a good fire could be made. Still it was hard to heat the room all over and I usually filled a $\frac{1}{2}$ gallon jug with water and put [it] to Jimmie's feet or sometimes when he went to sleep up by his hands to keep him warm enough. But some of us held him near the stove a good deal.

He was certainly the best natured happiest loving little mortal I have ever seen. I never spoke to him that he did not give me a bright smile even though he had been crying which he very seldom did. His papa or I would say "Jimmie jot little tot" and the smile was always there. He used to stand up straight as a poker on his father's hand while J.T. would dance around the room with him. He used to do this after church while I got Willie's things on and the women used to cry out in alarm that he would fall but I knew if he started to fall J.T. was quick enough to catch him. I made up a few verses about him but have forgotten all, but the first went like this:

> Standing erect on his father's hand
> Carelessly fearlessly looking down
> He stood like a child from fairy land
> As his father danced around and around.

And indeed he did look like a little fairy and many people seeing him would say "look at that little fairy." And Mr. Strohl said 40 years after "I wish your little boy that died could have lived to see what kind of a man he would make for he certainly had the finest head I ever saw on a child."

He used to lie long times on the bed but when he wanted to get up he would stick his feet up and wave them around and we would know he wanted up. We tried to get him to give his hands to be taken up and sometimes he would but mostly he gave his feet and we thought it rather a cute trick till it got me into trouble.

We went to Mayflower church one forenoon to hear my father preach and as we were a little late he had just started when we went in. That embarrassed me to start with. Aunt Hattie and Mrs. Wright made room for me to come back by them and I went carrying Jimmie and leading Willie. J.T. had carried Jimmie in but he stopped by the front of the house which was crowded. As soon as I sat down I laid Jimmie flat down on my lap and commenced to unbundle Willie. Aunt Hattie and then Mrs. Wright began to snicker and one to nudge another till just as I got Willie unbundled and fixed on his seat I looked around and Jimmie was lying waving his little red stockinged feet around in the air and wanting to get up. Of course I righted him but by that time one had nudged another and so on till everyone saw and my father stopped and said "They say there is a time to laugh and this seems to be the time" and everybody roared. I felt about as embarrassed as I ever did or could and it was a long time before I heard the last of it.

There are not many living now who were there but Aunt Hattie asked me last year if I ever learnt which end of a baby went up and my father laughed about it just before he died. I may hear of it again. I never could make them believe I had not carried him wrong end up.

In February I put in the early garden radishes lettuce peas onions parsnips carrots and beets and J.T. harrowed and got ready to sow wheat. Of course it snowed afterward and froze hard but nothing hurt the early garden and it was so much earlier than [that of] the neighbors who "waited till spring" that I always tried to get garden in in February whenever the ground could be worked and it has always been a success. Of course some years it is impossible but if ground is plowed in the fall it helps to get things started early.

I think it was along in March that Brother Summers and family came and spent the day with us. I had a good dinner cooked [and] the babies were well and good and everything was enjoyable. We had got to think a lot of these friends by now and when they mentioned that they had a number of cows they wished to put out on a three years' lease for one-half the increase we sat up and took notice. We asked a good many questions and finally told them we would think and talk it over and let them know as soon as we decided. Of course if they found someone else as they intimated they might before we decided why go ahead. They but especially she dilated at great length on the virtues and great value of their cows, something extra superior to all of them. I forget the number now but think it was eight.

Well we talked it over and over. J.T. hesitated on account of the extra work it would make [for] me though neither of us had any idea of what that would be. Well it seemed that with the wonderful amount of butter we would make according to Sister Summers we would be able to get all the groceries and dry goods we could use and at the end of 3 years have quite a little herd of cattle besides and from such wonderful milkers too. So about the last of March we went in to see about it and look at the cattle etc. We were both quite disappointed in their looks as they were quite thin but Mrs. Summers reminded us it was hard to keep good milkers in flesh. Neither of us knew a good milk cow by sight. Still we were not very favorably impressed especially as only one was giving any milk and she was nearly dry. But they were all to come fresh soon and would then give a bucketful apiece, so said sister Summers and he did not contradict.

Well taking their word against our judgment which we knew might not be very good we agreed to take them, and Brother Summers went to take out the papers and she called him into the kitchen and they had quite a little talk and when he came back he stated they thought it best to date the papers May 1st. That would give us a little over 3 years but was the time herds opened etc. and we agreed all right.

In fact, we had such confidence in them we would have agreed to most anything they proposed. So we went home and J. T. and Fred went after the cows and brought them home and great hopes we had though Fred said right off he did not believe they were very good milk cows. The oldest mother cow seemed part short horn but the best looking milkers seemed to be part Cherokee. However what could a boy know against the word of two such good friends as Brother and Sister Summers who knew just what they could and would do. All but a couple of 2 year olds going to have their first calves were large sized cows and the amount of good hay they ate before May 1st was a caution. They had been fed mostly straw all winter and tried to make up for it now, also the amount of water they drank which J. T. had to draw by windlass (as Fred went home when needed for spring work).

But still we hoped and planned until about the 2nd or 3rd of May we went to Juniata to do some trading but especially to get ropes for the cows. J. T. estimated that with 100 feet of rope apiece and changed every day or twice a day the cows would not know but what they were free as the grass would be just as good. We did not stop to think what a work it would be to change so many long ropes and how far it would soon take us from home and water. We went to Brother Summers to dinner and I took them some fresh eggs and probably other things, certainly more than enough to have bought our dinner. And the first thing they wanted to know was how many calves we had and when we said none yet they looked at one another in a way we did not understand then but afterwards we found they thought we were lying. When I was helping her in the kitchen later she said again "So none of the cows have calves. Very queer, very, they should have all had calves before now." And of course I told her how disappointed I had been that they had not, as butter would be a better price than after it got hot and easier to make good butter. But it seemed they did not believe us and in a few days they drove out to dinner and to see the cattle and none of them had calves yet and looked them over and said "I don't understand it at all."

We did not either then but we understood a plenty later. Some of the cows came in the latter part of May and some in June but we soon found that if any of them gave a bucket full of milk it had to be a real small bucket. And think of the terrible work for so very little milk and not much cream on the milk either. As Fred said, the Cherokee was the best of the bunch and she was only part civilized. They had always been herded and knew nothing of being staked on a rope and would stand on the end of the rope and weave back and forth till they would sometimes pull up the stake pin and in order to keep them from doing that I had to drive the stakes in so hard that sometimes I could not get them out and had to have J.T. come when he could and help me. And all the calves were staked out too and it took all J.T.'s spare time to draw water and to carry milk and water too.

And often I could hardly haul them to the house for water. They would hold back so on the rope till most there and then make a charge and drag me all over the yard. So by the time I had them watered and stakes changed in the morning I would be so exhausted I could hardly reach the house and there was that blessed baby not a thing to eat since I got up and looking up smiling all over to see me.

As J.T. was in the field he never knew how hard I worked. And I would not dare let [Jimmie] nurse till I cooled off a little and yet I suppose I nursed him too soon. Every week I seemed to get poorer and weaker and as the weather got hot and flies bad the cows got worse and worse acting. J.T. had to come to the rescue many times and did all he could without giving up the farm work entirely but it was too much after all.

There was a good deal of sickness among the babies in the neighborhood but we stayed at home. Fred came to help harvest and though we knew Jimmie was not well we did not think it anything serious till one day all of a sudden we got scared and sent to Juniata for Dr. Ackley and when he came and looked him over baby looked up at him and smiled and I thought he would say we did not need to call him but he said "I am sorry but it is too late to do anything now."

We were dumbfounded stupefied and as he was a young doctor then we thought he did not know. He left us something of course and said something about while there was life there was always a little hope and went away. But alas he knew too well. Old Lady Strohl, Jim's mother, came up to stay with us. I suppose Fred went home and told them on the way how sick the baby was. I could not let him out of my arms all night and in the morning with a look of love and [a] bright smile he was gone. He looked in my eyes and smiled and looked up over my head and smiled as if he saw something fine and I felt that he went from my arms to my mother's. I told Mrs. Strohl and she said "Might be, might be." She wanted to wash and dress him but I could not allow anyone else to touch my baby and so washed dressed him for the last time putting on him a little embroidered dress and skirt my mother made for me. Without my knowing it Aunt Hattie, I suppose, cut a piece out of the back of each and gave me afterwards which I still have.

We buried him in the yard. We could not take our baby away too far and a great many came to the burial that I never saw before or since. It seemed to me many thought it a holiday of some sort and the women acted very curious regarding everything in the house. I had a fine bedspread my mother had made on the bed and everything fixed up as good as possible and I guess they meant all right but to me nothing mattered but that the baby was gone from our lives and I could not bear to see folks act so concerned with every little thing. I soon found I could not stand up. My limbs would not support me and I had to spend several days in bed while the men folks got along with the harvest and cows and made out the best they could.

They got Vernie Barnhart to come and do some cooking but I got around in a few days though nothing seemed to matter much. J.T. was as heartbroken as I was but someone had to look after things and as I failed to rally he had to keep things going. All he could say was "We have each other and one boy left." But we knew then as always that if we had a thousand babies no one would or could take Jimmie's place.

I suppose I might have lain and grieved myself to death had it not been for the shock about the pigs. The young sow we had got from Father the year before in exchange for our bloodthirsty one had 7 fine pigs that spring and as I took delight in seeing anything grow vegetable or animal so I rejoiced in them. I had J.T. fix a swill barrel as Grandpa Smith had and into it poured milk and dishwater and some shorts as near like he did as I could remember and let it ferment. I also pulled weeds and whatever green stuff I could sweet corn stalks and etc. and J.T. helped and we took great pride in our pigs.

Well either Fred and J.T. were putting up hay or else had gone to help Father with his harvest. Anyway they were away all day and I lay quiet and felt rather cold all day. Along in the afternoon Vernie came in and said "My it is a hot day. The worst yet." I thought she was joking but saw she was not [and] then said "Vernie run and see how the pigs are" for they were getting so big the shade over the pen was hardly big enough but I had always kept watch of them before. Now I had forgotten them. She came back and reported "3 of them are dead and the rest panting awful." "Oh go quick" I said "and take down the pen," telling her how to hurry and drive them into some shade either the house or barn or wherever you can get them the quickest. She was gone it seemed a long time but came back and said they were in the shade and she thought would get all right.

This kind of shocked me awake and I began to look around. I saw Willie trying to play around and keep still with a new serious look in his eyes. Poor little fellow he missed his little playmate and we had neglected him. I felt guilty now indeed and called him to come to me and comforted him. When J.T. came home and heard about the pigs he did not seem to care [and] said [he] guessed there were enough left [and] that I looked a little better and that was all he cared. Oh I told him I was a lot better and wanted to sit up and eat supper with him which pleased him wonderfully though he did not know whether I ought to or not. In fact neither of us knew much about ourselves or how to take care of ourselves and it took a long time to learn. So the next morning I got up and walked a little and saw how the chickens and garden and flowers needed me to say nothing of Willie and J.T. who looked ten years younger so I think he had been doing a lot of worrying.

We let Vernie go and the men folks did all the hard work for a long time but your father said if I would just stick around where he could look at me it was all he cared. Some neighbors, Cline, had moved into the ¼ section joining us on the north that spring. They were old settlers in the country and used to live near Kenesaw. The oldest son Lansing came down one day to see Fred and be neighborly and after being there a while said "I see you have the old Summers outfit of cows."

"Yes what do you know about them?"

"Well I know a plenty. I ran the town herd for Juniata last year and they were in it and made more trouble than all the rest together. That old brindled grandmother was always traipsing off and would fairly run a pony to death just for orneriness and I don't believe one of them ever gave enough milk to pay for milking, at least they gave no sign of it. And the calves ran with most of them and did not get much. How do you find them?"

And we knew the boy was telling the truth and that Mrs. Summers had lied most outrageously to get rid of paying herdage for the cattle. If they had told us the truth that they were not good to milk and most of them never had been we might have taken them and put them in the country herd at $1.00 a head to raise their calves but we had bought more rope than they were worth to try to make milk cows of them.

Sometime along probably the middle of August Summers his wife and family came out to see us or the cattle and first we could not act very pleased as we were sore at our treatment but I had no idea of the volcano that had been slumbering in the breast of your father. When they had exclaimed over our bad looks and Summers said something about losing our baby he simply erupted into the air. "Yes and before God you murdered him" he said "and nearly killed my wife besides and if she had died you would better have looked out."

Then he told him in wild language how he had lived for years at the end of the R.R. track towns filled with tin horn gamblers saloon keepers and men of the lowest class but had never before associated with a d——d liar. Even to insinuate that a man was that meant to die in 15 seconds unless you were quickest on the draw. Then he told him what he was in no uncertain terms and I though somewhat shocked knew that every word was true and very appropriate. He ended by saying that if his cows had not been better Christians than he was we would have raised a lot of 3 year olds for nothing.

Really I don't think until then he hardly believed himself that they had deliberately tried to cheat us by dating the papers May 1st which would make us keep all the present herd 3 years for ½ the increase but Mrs. spoke up and gave it all away saying he ought to "look out what he signed, everyone must look out for their own interest." Then another slighter eruption and J.T. said "Well I wanted you to acknowledge before my wife that you were a pair of unmitigated blank ——— liars who would deceive and doublecross your best friends for a little money and you," turning to Summers, who had knelt with arm around him at times in eloquent prayer for help and strength to avert temptation, "*you* knew I was trying to do right and you ought to have helped me instead of pitching me into Hell like this."

And he went outdoors and Summers soon followed. I was too dumbfounded to say a word and I guess Mrs. Summers was ashamed.

After awhile the men came in and announced the cattle would go back right away. J.T. wanted to take the whole lot back but I believe Summers insisted we keep one or 2 of the young steers. We did not want heifers.

This might not be worth recording except for its far-reaching effects. I do not think your father ever entered a church again except for a funeral or some special occasion. As for me though

I could not blame all ministers or church people as he did for so long I knew I was going with him. If he went to Church or Heaven I wanted to go but if to the other place I still wanted to be along.

Fred and J.T. drove the stock to Juniata and turned them into the corral. I do not think they spoke to anyone and we never met them again. Neither did we speak of it to anyone or even often to ourselves as J.T. always said "That is past history now." But I wish I had gone to Aunt Hattie and Father and Mrs. Wright and told them the truth of it because I know Mrs. Summers told them things against us but I never knew just what. If we had and Uncle Chester and O.H. had told Mr. Kellie as they would have that they thought as little as he of such doings life might have been different for us in many ways.

But we kept still and about the next thing we knew Father got ready and moved to Kearney and took Fred along and left John in Juniata to work for his board at Summers' and go to school. Summers evidently had made Father think he was all right and I suppose he wanted John there or rather she did so folks would think my folks sided with them. I felt dreadful bad to have Johnny go to live with them after finding what they were but J.T. said "Oh don't worry about Johnny. He will be all right. He is a good boy [and] they can't hurt him. Liars have to be born not made and no son of your Mother and Father either could be a liar."

I don't remember much about our crops that fall. Guess they were not very bad or very good and of course we thought it would be better when we got more ground in but to do that [we] would have to have another horse and more machinery. Sometime that summer or fall they built a large sod barn so we could keep more freighters that winter and put up a lot of hay. Oh they were always busy 14 and even 16 hours a day until we thought someday we would get a start and rest.

I do not know what started Father off to Kearney. His wife made some kind of a row and they went but what he intended to do or did do there I do not know and don't think I ever did but think some kind of team work. But before a great while we heard Fred had gone, disappeared, run away, anyway gone and I looked for him to come to our place and Father thought he would so it was the first place he looked and I suppose Fred knew it would be. He could not get along with his stepmother and she wanted him to go, at least it seemed so she did. I watched and watched every night and every day, sure Fred would come but no Fred and then we heard John had left Summers' and no one knew where he was and I watched for him also and probably it was good in a way that I had something besides my great grief to worry about. We missed the boys who had been with us so much as when not with us they were always coming up Sundays to see us.

Aunt Sophy had been sending the boys the Youth's Companion for awhile and they used to bring it up and have me read it aloud. They often read it before but liked to have me read it and J.T. and I greatly enjoyed it also. The house was so lonesome I hated to be in it a minute so tagged J.T. around whenever I had time but as winter set in the freighters came so often that we were never alone at night and usually some were there to feed their teams and get their dinner. We did not go to church or anywhere else that winter till along in January I think J.T. drove to Hastings on business and came home after dark and there was Johnny with him.

My but I was overjoyed and I guess he was as glad to get back. Though he never said much he wore his usual contented grin. He was a little short fellow for his age and J.T. found him on the street blacking boots. He was making his living but that was about all. Only J.T. said every man in town seemed to be his friend [and] all had a pleasant or jolly greeting for him. Johnny never would say very much why he ran away from Summers'. He was no hand to talk much anyway. Took his talk most all out in whistling. We always knew where he was by his jolly whistle. But I knew how very anxious he had been to go to school so coaxed at him till he finally said that he did not object at all to taking all the care of the team and the cows and chickens but it got so he had to wash all the dishes and they would be gone 2 and 3 days at a time and did not leave him much to eat and did not get up in the morning in time so he could get to school until late and finally she got to making him mop the floor and well he just could not manage that old mop to suit her and so he concluded to quit. I never knew anyone more anxious for an education than he or who learnt easier. What a difference it would have made in his and all our lives if he could [have] continued on in school.

So Johnny sat by the wood box and kept it whittled full of stalks and did all kinds of chores, taking good care of the hens so we got eggs every day which few of the neighbors did and as [during] the winter before we had good cash sale[s] for them to the freighters.

But before Johnny came back Mr. Strohl had lent to us a couple of books of Bob Ingersoll's and some other of like nature which his brother-in-law Yoetom of Hastings had sent out. I read them aloud to J. T. and although we did not take very much stock in them as there was nothing to believe, as it seems to me now it amounted to the fact that Ingersoll did not know anything and did not believe anyone else did. Still they were written in flowery language and had an effect that was greater at this time than would have been at any other, the effect of destroying or injuring our faith and hope and everything good without giving anything in return. For the first time since I could remember I could not say "I *know* that my redeemer liveth and because he lives I shall live also." I had been so thoroughly taught this that a doubt had never entered my mind before, now when I needed this faith as never before came this eloquent infidel to destroy it. Still of course it was not destroyed entirely but doubt enough entered in to take the happiness out of religion and more or less from life. Strohl was as good a neighbor as one could have a smart and fascinating personality who would die before he would injure a neighbor knowingly yet in lending those books he did more to injure our happiness than any other person.

After Johnny came he lent us Tom Sawyer and then Roughing It, both of which I read aloud to the delight of all and sometimes the freighters heard part of them and the comments they made etc. made the evenings pass quite pleasantly. For those tired men who had tramped all day long beside their wagons in the snow without overshoes [and were] now in beside a good fire thawing out their wet and frozen boots greatly enjoyed something that gave them a good hearty laugh. So Mark Twain's nonsensical sense brought cheer and happiness to many that winter while Bob Ingersoll's sensible nonsense brought heartache and woe.

The pictures that stand out most in looking over memories

of that winter are John sitting on the wood box whittling stalk and telling stories to Willie and taking him on his back for a run in the snow, John bundling Willie up and setting him on the scoop shovel and running like a deer all over the yard in the snow [with] Willie laughing with glee, and the freighters' wagons creaking in the snow, always coming and going creaking in the snow. We must have had a long and snowy winter.

That fall Aunt Susie had written from Madison, Wisconsin, that Cousin Charlie Smith and his brother and mother and stepfather and family had moved to Nebraska somewhere at a place called Minden. We inquired around a good deal but no one knew what part of the state that was in so I wrote a letter and told him our section, town, range, and post office which I think was then Mayflower as Griswolds ran the P.O. then.

A letter soon came back giving their location also and the information that Minden was the new county seat of Kearney County and our farms were only about 13 miles apart. And after a little Charlie came over to see us on horseback and urged us to come to see them. He had taken a homestead and so had [his brother?] Willie but both of them were living most of the time with their mother as they did not like batching.

So after John came we all got ready one day and drove over and stayed all night and came back the next day and let the freighters run the ranch to suit themselves which they did as we found some money on the table and everything all right. We had a good visit and it seemed good to be with old friends again. They seemed glad to see us so it made a pleasant time all around.

Cousin Charlie was my mother's brother William's boy. William died in the civil war and Charlie lived a good number of years with Grandpa Smith or Aunt Susie. As we lived with Grandpa Smith also through the civil war Charlie and I were a good deal like brother and sister. His mother was a very peculiar woman and married again a young soldier who went in at the last of the war so was a good many years younger than herself. He is still living at Minden but I see a grandson of his lately died in the navy. Well Aunt Deborah as we called her believed in bringing her young husband up right and was constantly scolding him for doing something or not doing something, all of which he took in the utmost good humor.

When we went to see them the first thing Mr. Kellie picked me out of the wagon and set me down she said "Now see Joe that is the way you ought to do." We all kept straight faces but as she weighed 250 or so and he about 150 we could hardly manage to do so. Then every time J.T. showed me any courtesy or politeness or attended to Willie or anything she would say "Now see Joe that is the way you ought to do." Till really I was afraid to look at J.T. or John for fear of laughing right out and I believe J.T. spread his politeness on a little thicker than common to hear her say "Now see Joe" etc.

And after we went home John would frequently cry out as he saw any sign of gallantry or love "Now see Joe" till it became a great byword with him. And when that spring they came to pay our visit back she was still scolding Joe and cross about it too and every little while it was "Now see Joe" to Johnny's great delight. Finally the worm turned and Joe said "Now see Deborah why don't you be like Luna? I have never heard her give him a cross word yet."

"Ah" said Deborah in a gleeful tone "she don't have to. While you keep me wore out he never does anything for her to be cross about."

And then, that is one of the things I like to remember, J.T. put his arm around me and said "God knows I do, many of them, but she has never given me a cross word or look yet. I don't know why."

So I said "That is easy. I never *felt* cross at you yet." So however cross and cranky I may have got in after years I like to remember I was not always so and it was not hard work to keep from being [cross] for I never *felt* that way.

That fall I wanted to get a lot of outing flannel and flannel or winter clothes and had a couple of 3 gallon jars of good solid butter to trade on it. I had taken one crock full to Kenesaw and got $12\frac{1}{2}$ cents a pound for it and the flannel was 15 cents a yard but we had heard a good deal about Hastings being a good place to trade. So when we found a young unmarried neighbor Charles Kidd, a nephew of Powers, was going to Hastings for lumber to build a sod house J.T. spoke for a chance for me to go with him. He came real early in the morning as Powers was with him and he had to be in Hastings by 9 o'clock to serve on a Jury. So I went with them with my 2 jars of butter. I found out however that they would only pay 10 cents a pound for butter. They did not look at mine but that was all they could pay for any they said and when I priced their flannel it was 18 cents a yard for the same quality as was 15 at Kenesaw. So I took my butter back home to take to Kenesaw.

And as soon as Charles Kidd loaded up his lumber we started for home. But his load was heavy and the lumber came up above the double wagon box and went back several feet behind the wagon bed, so we only got opposite the old depot and on the south side of the track on the section line where the road ran before the Asylum was located when a tire came off a wheel. So he unhitched his team and took them away and took the wheel to a blacksmith shop to be fixed. I went into the depot to wait and had to wait a very long time as I suppose the smith was busy and Kidd had to wait his turn. While waiting I asked the agent about bridge building and told him my husband was a bridge framer and foreman on construction and he said he knew they were short of good bridge men and told where to apply.

The sun was real low when we got started again and with the heavy load we had to go slow but that was not the worst. The lumber stuck out so far behind that it kept working back and [was] in danger of sliding back altogether so we had to unload a time or two before we got to Juniata.

We drove up into the town ½ mile out of the way to get Mrs. Burns who was visiting there. She came out with her baby and satchel and some things she had bought. One I remember was a large shank of beef. We had not gone far before the load worked back again and we had to unload. We were up real high you know so this was about the performance. Charlie [Kidd] got down and we handed him the spring seat and the satchel the other bundles [and] the soup bone. I took the baby and he helped Mrs. Burns down. I gave him the baby to give Mrs. Burns, then the jars of butter and boxes of nails etc. he had bought and the quilts. Then he helped me down. Then he unloaded all that big load of lumber and reloaded it while Mrs. Burns and I sat and wanted to laugh and I guess we did pretty frequently. And yet we felt sorry and half expected Charlie would get mad or make some fuss having such a time with 2 old married women along. But he kept good natured all the time and it did not discourage him from getting married soon after. Well we reloaded in about the same order and I am sure I do not know how often it occurred but it was about morning when we reached home and I found a very worried husband. I wanted him to apply for a bridge position but he was so emphatic in his refusal that I never referred to the matter again.

One of the freighters that winter had a large roast of Buffalo meat with him and cut off quite a slice for us. It was a tame one he had raised from a calf and had got to be about 3 years old but so unruly he could not build a pen that would hold it or a fence that would keep it out of his garden and crops. He told us several funny things about it but finally he had to kill it. We did not fancy the meat. It was so dark and dry, still it was tender and fat enough.

This was the year [1879] the Ponca [Cheyenne] Indians made their raid through the southwestern part of the state to get back to their old homes. The government had removed them to Oklahoma where they nearly all sickened and many died and they started for home. Several of the freighters lived near where they went and saw ruins of buildings they had burnt and told of people they killed.

One day one of the freighters going to Hastings with a load of wheat said he was to meet his wife's sister there who had come from Philadelphia to see them. She had never been west before and had lived in the city all her life and he did not know how she would stand it going home about 4 days' drive on a lumber wagon of groceries for one of the stores. However he said she was a nice woman and he always liked her and he thought she would be game and said he would like to bring her there to stay all night the next night but one. So though desperately afraid of eastern city people who had never even seen a sod house we told him to come ahead and J.T. said she could sleep with me and he would sleep on the floor, which I guess was the reason he had told us, as though he carried some extra quilts this trip he hated to put her on the cold floor with strange men around.

So I had everything as shiny as I could. We ate our supper early and I had the tea kettle boiling and everything ready when they came. I don't think anyone else was there that night as his crowd did not come as this was kind of an extra trip on account of her coming. So I put on a tablecloth for them and [took] some of my dishes down for them to use as they [the freighters] only took old tin dishes which I thought would be rough for her.

She was a very pleasant young woman and although everything about her clothes travelling bag etc. denoted wealth she did not make any pretense of superiority or act like a tenderfoot. You might have thought she had lived in a one room sod house all her life by her fine manners. She had a large wicker lunch basket packed with most delicious eatables but said she had not felt hungry for cold lunch so had not eaten much of it. Fried chicken and Jells and Jams and cakes of various kinds as well as fresh fruits made a lunch fit for anyone. But our freighter friend teased her about everything and fried some pork and got some eggs from me and showed her how to make real coffee in his old black coffee pot [and] showed her what a grand cook he had got to be since coming west.

She praised his cooking and she gave Willie some fruit and chicken which he [the freighter] hoped would not make him sick and finally she offered him a piece of frosted marble cake, the white so very white and black so very black that I think it must have had chocolate in it but had never seen any chocolate then. He said to Willie "Look out, see she never washed her hands before she made it. Just look at the black streaks." And Willie refused to take it and backed off and looked very earnestly at her and the cake and she said "Take it. He is fooling, it is all right." He said "Ha Ha, to make a cake a child will not eat." And she was embarrassed and so was I so I told Willie to go get it, it was fine but he looked at it and at the man and would not go. And he laughed and carried on till she told him wait till she got him home where her sister would make him behave.

But I think he was trying to keep her from getting homesick for he was good to her as he could be [and] warmed stones to put to her feet for she could not run in the snow with him [and] he had to keep her warm other ways. They must have taken her to Kearney when they went back for she said they would sure stop if they came that way. But it was nearer to Kearney if they did not have any freighting to do. So that made a bright spot in our lives to have a real lady act like a friend.

John and I had a great time with the seed catalogues that winter especially Burpee's. He would make out a list and I would add to it or change it and I would make one and he would change it. J.T. was interested and added several things to be sure to have plenty of carrots and peas but he could not get up so much enthusiasm over the prospect of gardening as John and I. We could not get things in as early on account of the snow but we made plans and got our seeds ready. Lots of onion seed for John said he could tend them and in fact lots of everything. I had saved some seeds but we ordered more and could hardly wait to get to work.

I must tell about our pigs. The 4 that lived did fine and we killed some of them when about 300 days old. We had no way of weighing them live but dressed they averaged 325 pounds which we thought did fine. We fried out lots of lard and smoked the hams and shoulders and though new to the business I have never tasted better. So our cellar was filled with good meat and lard for all summer. I think we kept it all except some we sold to the freighters.

Spring was just opening up and we had been putting in early garden when nearly sundown one afternoon when we saw a strange outfit pulling into the yard. It was a small homemade wagon about 2 feet wide by 4 or 5 long with a canvas cover and drawn by a man and woman. And inside was a little curly haired girl about 4 years old and a baby 6 or 8 months with their clothing some bedding and camping utensils. The man was rather tall and slim and sober faced, the woman short fat and jolly. He was quite a bit older than she.

She introduced themselves in a laughing manner as Mr. and Mrs. Sam Ship from the coal mines of Pennsylvania and on their way to a homestead in Phelps County. Said they had walked all the way or Sam had as sometimes going down easy places she rode and going up hill she pulled and most times they both pulled together. They wished to stay all night and of course we made them welcome. She offered to buy milk for the children and eggs and said they had never begged although they left home with almost nothing. When they got out of money they stopped and one or other or both worked until they got ahead enough to go a ways farther. They had been over 2 years on the road. The baby they had when they started had been buried on the way and this one was born on the road but nothing daunted the mother who was fairly radiant for joy of being near their journey's end where they could have a home of their own.

We naturally gave them all the milk, butter, eggs and some other things they could use for supper and breakfast and some to take along and enjoyed visiting with them. Anyone with pluck enough to cross the Alleghenies and [go] on to have a home sure deserved what help we had to offer. And she was good company. I remember one of the first things she said. "My father is Irish and my mother is a Dutchman." She said all their friends who worked in the mines lived in rented houses and never had a home or garden or anything or place to raise chickens pigs or any livestock and were not better off at the end of one year than the year before.

So when she and Sam got married they resolved to save all they could and as soon as they could get the money would go west and get them a real home. But one year after another passed and they had no more money than the year before. "So finally I told Sam" she said "that we might just as well start if we were ever going as we would never get any better able than we were then." But he said they could not go without money to pay fare etc.

"Why we will walk" she said.

"We can't walk so far" he said "and the children can't walk at all."

"Well Sam" she said "we must walk if we ever go and we are going to go so you build a stout little wagon to put the children in and what few things we have to have and we will take what money the furniture brings and start and when we run out of money we will work. It may take quite a while but we will get there and it is the only way we ever will." She said he was hard to convince but finally she had her way and they started.

"And now" she said "here we are." Sam had left her to work in Hastings while he went out afoot and located a homestead in Phelps County and put up a small sod house so they felt they were indeed almost home.

In the morning when they started on I gave her the little

blue morocco shoes of Willie's for her baby. They were real good yet as I had protected them so much with cloth shoes over [and] they looked nearly new. Also gave her a trio of white chickens. These were a cross from a white bantam hen crossed twice with Brahma so they were quite large size but pure white with smooth yellow legs. A good deal like the White Rocks of today. But I wanted to keep only pure Brahmas so we had been eating these white ones though they were fine layers. We had only two hens and one buck left so I boxed them up for them early in the morning and when we went out after breakfast there was an egg laid and my what a fuss the little girl made over it and the woman most as bad. Her father came to see us 3 or 4 years afterwards. He was Irish all right straight from the old sod so I suppose her mother was a Dutchman. He said they had the farm literally covered with pure white fowls all from the ones we had given them and that she often spoke of us and wanted us to come and see them.

After the grasshoppers had killed Father's young orchard in '76 he planted a lot of apple seeds Richardson sent out from his cider mill in Wisconsin. They grew nicely and he now had a nice bunch of two year olds and told us to come and get all we wanted as they were too thick and more than he cared for. So we laid out an orchard that spring and set out about 100 of them. Also Aunt Hattie gave us a quantity of strawberry plants and some lilacs and roses from Grandpa Sanford's old place in Wisconsin and we set a couple long rows of wild plums from choice seed Strohl raised from selected wild plums. So with our garden and chickens we were all busy. J.T. set most of the trees but mostly he did the farm work and John and I the garden.

Willie of course was an interested listener of our talks about raising things. Just how interested we did not realize until later. I had a box of many assorted buttons, some common and some quite fine ones my aunts had sent me saying they might come useful and one day I noticed it was nearly empty.

"Why where are my buttons?" Silence. "Has anybody seen my buttons?"

"Not I." "Not I," from J.T. and Johnny.

"Willie have you had my buttons?"

"Yes."

"Where are they?"

"Outdoors."

"Where outdoors? Go and get them right away."

"I can't."

"Why not?"

"I planted them."

"Planted them for land sakes why did you plant them?"

"I wanted me some garden too."

So I went with him and we dug up probably half of them. But as he evidently wanted to raise nice ones the finest ones were planted and some were shallow and some deep and as it had rained the tracks were pretty well covered up so many of them are still there I suppose.

We had only 3 teaspoons bought when there were only 2 of us and now we had to borrow from one another. So one day I only could find one. Close questioning revealed the fact that Willie had planted them to raise more so we could all [have] one. I discovered the loss so soon that we were able to dig up the missing spoons without loss and try to explain to Willie that everything did not grow by planting it. But it seemed hard for him to draw the line and one day I found a sack of feathers I was saving for pillows had a lot gone out of it. Inquiries along the same line revealed that Willie had planted them so he could have a feather bed.

All this time whenever we saw a young man coming either afoot or horseback we always watched him closely to see if it could be brother Fred as we could not give up hope that he would come back. In that way we first saw the one we called the mysterious rider. A young man on a gray horse who went east in the afternoons and west the next morning early. We did not see him often but wondered who he could be as we knew he did not live near and he always kept his face turned to the south when passing, unless if cold or stormy he had a cape or blanket thrown over his head. J.T. and John thought it might be Charlie Smith and that he did not want to stop and so did not want us to recognize him but I was very sure that Charlie would not go by and not stop. Father came down from Kearney that spring and put in some crop and on one trip took Willie home with him for a day or two where he had a great time as nothing was too good for Grandpa's boy.

We had a great abundance of eggs and used them in a great many ways and it seemed we did not tire of them. They were so cheap it hardly paid to try to sell them, often 6 and sometimes 3 cents a dozen, so we used all we wanted and set the rest and soon the place was swarming with young chickens. Aunt Sophy sent me some things this spring and among others several Harper's magazines. One of them told of the wonders to be seen along the Yellowstone River (now park) and [had] several pictures of them, and the tales of hot geysers and all the wonderful things interested us greatly. We made up our minds we were going to see all those wonderful things for ourselves. We planned we would take a vacation before many years. Find someone to look after the farm and take a team and take a summer trip up there. John was eager to go with us. We all worked hard all day and as we got up early so we went to bed early but not to sleep. Oh no, to talk about our trip to the Yellowstone. John and Willie slept in the same room so we all talked in the dark together. We agreed Frank and Bill were an ideal team, light and good travellers. We must get a light wagon [and] then decide what to take. One night we would plan to take a lot of stuff and almost decide to take two teams. The next we would cut out a lot of it and decide to live on the game of the country mostly. Our trip never materialized but we put in some happiest hours of life planning it.

This spring an oldish man and a young one from Kentucky came along on their way west. They had heard of the Indian trouble the fall before and as they were going a long ways west were expecting they might meet trouble. J.T. had traded my revolver off, with my consent of course, for a large rifle carrying a one ounce ball I believe. It certainly would be a wicked weapon but there was nothing here we needed it for. But he had made a place to hang it over the door [and] in case it was ever needed we had it ready.

This young man had a beautiful long rifle the prettiest firearm I ever saw, silver plate inset and bright brass patch box. It took a very small bullet so he thought it would not be much use for Indians. He asked J.T. how he would trade and they took both rifles out and shot at marks. The young man was fine shot and J.T. said he never thought anyone could shoot like he did and while he said of course the Kentucky rifle was worth much more than ours we could not afford to give boot[?] as we had not much use for either.

So he told him to take his choice and he would take one down and then put it up and take down the other. He hated to part with his rifle and we did nothing to influence him. We would have sold him ours cheap and offered to but I think he did not have any extra money perhaps. Anyway he started to go with his own rifle at last, then turned quickly and came back and took down the other one saying he supposed a man's life was worth more than a rifle. So we had that lovely rifle which was an ornament to any room and as the ammunition cost little J.T. got to be a great shot with it and woe to any rabbit he pointed it at.

After that we often took the team and drove off around the prairie just after sunset and J.T. would shoot a number of rabbits for the chickens to eat. Hungry as we had often been for meat we could neither of us stand it to eat rabbit meat and indeed it was not fit to eat, it still seems to me, as it was so dark and dry and tough. Some of the rabbits of those days must have been very old I think. But as soon as there got to be corn fields for them to feed in and plenty of grassland not burnt off they got to be very palatable eating. And now nice young rabbit meat, corn fed and raised near an alfalfa field, is hard to beat or equal.

We had been fortunate in getting our first team that though small they [were] very spry and willing and [had] a good trusty affectionate disposition. But as they were not large enough to pull a goodsized breaker or other plow alone we had to have a third plow and that was where trouble began as J.T. fell among thieves or a more polite name horse dealers and I cannot recall the various horses he had and all their faults and diseases. One I think the first one broke out with button farcy (heat pimples, button farcy is glanders) as soon as he tried to work and got his blood heated up. He was young and a fine looking horse but worthless to work and the one we had this spring was balky by spells and the spells came frequently and were quite unpleasant to deal with.

This was the spring Richards was hung at Minden for the murder of a man where he was working and he had murdered a woman and 3 children the fall before but never had his trial for that. The day of the hanging I do not think any one went from our neighborhood but a number drove by from Hastings. J.T. was plowing close to the road in front of the house and John and I [were] at the garden by the house when the horse took a notion to balk, threw its head around, tangled itself up I suppose and threw itself flat on the ground. Just then and before we could start to help several teams drove up from Hastings, the first a carriage with prancing horses and 4 men. The driver checked up and called out "How will you trade horses?"

"Oh go on" said J.T. "I have just as poor a team as I want." The fellow drove on with a cut of the whip and yells of pure joy from his companions and the teams behind.

And then just before harvest an awful thing happened. Right in the middle of the night there were some hard claps of thunder and another awful sound of breaking timber and falling sods. J.T. called out "All out quick, the house is falling down." We were all on our feet in a flash though I was so frightened I guess I would have lain there if he had not hollered. He said "Come here to Willie. Lift one end." John usually so hard to wake had tumbled out. J.T. took one end of the bed tick Willie was lying on and we rushed outdoors. I was really too frightened to remember much but Will says about his earliest recollection is his father and me carrying his bed around outdoors and it was going to rain and we were questioning each other where to put it, whether to go in the barn or stay out in the rain. He was very anxious to have us take him back in the house so he could go back to sleep. I think we decided on the barn till the storm was over but I felt I never wanted to sleep under a roof again. I thought it was the world coming to an end till J.T. hollered. And it sure was an end to many hopes for we had never finished the house but expected to that fall. We had been so sure that great log and all those heavy timbers would last as long as we would want a sod house and it had been nice and cozy and now we were turned out in the dark wet night so suddenly that a very few clothes were all we had till we could dig them out in daylight.

I know we spent some nights sleeping in a stall in the barn and I suppose that was one of them but I was desperately afraid by that time so every nice night we made our beds on the grass in the yard. We dug out our stuff, most of it all right, some wet and muddy. They carried the stove and table out in the yard and I cooked there while they harvested. I remember one night we were all tired and had gone to bed early. It was dark but too much wind for a lamp to burn well outdoors and we had nothing to read so went to bed and lay talking but about our trip to the Yellowstone I presume when Clarence and Hetty Griswold came riding up horseback. I don't think they had heard about the roof falling down as we were too busy to run around to tell the news and they rode up to the cook stove first thing and [were] surprised stopped and called hello. "Hello" said J.T. "what are you doing in the kitchen? But [it's] all right just so you don't come in the bedroom over this way." So we got up. They stopped and we visited awhile and we could laugh about it by that time serious as it was. We had got word that Father was moving back from Kearney onto his timber claim. Someone told us he had moved a small frame building down and was going to be moved by Sunday.

So Sunday after dinner as it was a very fine day we started to go over there. I had not been well enough to ride for all summer but thought I could go that far 3½ miles by the road and we followed the road that day by Old Man King's. Soon after we passed there a sudden storm came up. We hurried the team as soon as we saw it coming but it caught us on the bare prairie and it began to hail. And such hail, thick and fast and good sized too. The horses would not stand to face it but turned for home. J.T. took off his coat and put it over his and my head to protect us all he could while John and Willie crowded under the wagon seat for protection. But John wanted to see how large the hail was so popped out his head and one large one took him on the back of the head so with an "ouch" he was glad to get under again. When we got home he had a great big bump on his head which was sore for quite a long time. We made good time for home and dry clothes for we had put some clothes in the barn to keep dry but before we got home the sun was shining again. We heard afterwards that Father was not there for a day or two later so it was just as well we did not go on.

We had a wet harvest that year, at least many showers that delayed cutting, and they had to turn some of the shocks to dry them out. J.T. had bought a secondhand Marsh harvester the year before and I had driven it some while the men bound. It was one where 2 men rode and bound the grain and threw it off but this year I was not able to drive it and we hired Maran King. I remember he needed some work shirts and sent and bought some shirting and I made him 2 all by hand, back stiched all the seams and felled them and charged him 25 cents each and I was proud to think that I could help that much for I was so miserable. I had to sit to wash dishes and sit by the stove to keep a fire and cook. I would sit by the tub and do a good deal of the washing but John would bring and empty all the water and hang out the clothes and once or twice he took a lot of things down to the lagoon and washed and dried them there to suit himself. For men don't like to be bossed around when they have to do women's work.

Mrs. Strohl and Ann Manzer came to see me and both said I had ruined myself for life working in the broom corn while Jimmie was little and I thought they knew and shed many bitter tears. But one thing I never thought to do was to see any doctor about it. Doctor Williams must have come to Kenesaw along those times for I remember seeing him ride horseback by there sometimes but it never entered our heads to call him in. Folks did not call doctors those days, only for something serious.

I don't believe anyone ever hated to go in debt or ask for credit as bad as J.T. did. That was why we had gone hungry and cold when we could have mortgaged our cattle for food as some others did. But he had had to go in debt for the harvester. It was secondhand as I guess they were anxious to get it sold again so had given him a year's time and it was about time and he had it to worry over and the rain and me and everything. No wonder he got old young. But now he felt he must get lumber enough to put up a shed large enough to hold our beds at least so he plucked up courage and went to Kenesaw and got it all right and put up a shed room about 10 x 12.

And we were only in there a few days when we hurried John after Mrs. Manzer in the night and before morning on August 30th 1879 we had a fine little daughter. J.T. was in the 7th heaven of bliss at once. The nicest baby yet (every baby was always the nicest yet to J.T.) and a little daughter. He wanted to name it Luna but I had been plagued about my name so much when small that I did not want to give it to anyone else. So we called her Susie and she was a loving little thing who soon knew her papa and he always held her every minute he could spare and I hoped it would cure some of the hurt about Jimmie but one child can never take the place of another.

J.T. said I must stay in bed longer this time so I stayed about 4 days and then got up. I felt much better than for a long time and did not like to see the men messing around trying to cook when so much outside work was needing to be done. Very few hired a girl those days for such occasions but the man or family got along the best they could till the woman got around again.

So now we wanted to get the threshing done and out of the way fall plowing etc. etc. and I told them I could cook for the threshers as soon as they could get ready, for J.T. had to go to town and get some more lumber to enlarge the shed so we could set the table for threshers. So he fixed it up and John dug or plowed out a load of sweet potatoes which J.T. took to Kearney and brought back a lot of groceries and other needed things.

I think it was while he was at Kearney Mr. Linnegar of the firm of Linnegar and Metcalf a big machinery company came to see him about the payment on the binder I suppose for I don't see what else it could have been. We had been notified it was about due but could not do anything. J.T. simply had to fix the shed and some place to live and we did not know how much wheat we would have. Well they drove up (he had a driver who stayed in the buggy). Mr. Linnegar came in and introduced himself and asked for Mr. Kellie. I told him where he was. He saw the young baby and asked if it had been born there and how old it was and said I ought not to be out of bed.

He sat there and talked quite pleasantly so I felt quite at home with him and told him just how we were fixed, how much wheat to thresh, how we had to fix some kind of a house, and how afraid I was of sod houses. How J.T. had worried about the debt he owed them and expected to pay it soon as we could thresh and haul off the wheat, but wheat was low and it cost for threshing and we had to pay some for harvest. And in short he could see we would not have much to fix a house let alone get through the winter but I guess he felt we were honest for as he rose to go he said "Tell Mr. Kellie not to worry about the note to us. I will mark it extended for another year and tell him I want him to go ahead and fix up a better place for you and the baby before it gets cold." Can you wonder we always felt that that was a good firm to deal with.

One of the instances which must have happened that summer or fall was Johnny rushing in to tell me to come quick and see the buffalo. Going out and down to the road there was J.T. talking to the drivers who had stopped. They had the largest wagon I ever say piled up high with bales of wool and hauled by 3 or 4 yoke of oxen and one yoke of buffalo. That was a great sight for me as it was the first I had ever seen. Johnny and I looked them over from every direction and did not pay much attention to anything else, but J.T. who had seen lots of them on the plains in '68 when working on the U.P.R.R. visited with the men. He was always a great mixer and if he were alive could undoubtedly tell their names, where from, how long on the road and much else but all I saw was the buffalo which did not look much as I expected. Their heads were so shaggy and carried so low, their humps so large, shoulders so heavy and hind quarters so small. When they got to Juniata they sold the buffalo to Mr. Buer who I believe took them east with a show.

J.T. got home with the groceries tea, coffee, sugar, stuff for sauce and pies etc. The threshers agreed to come a certain day right away and I got busy so as to be able to handle the work alone. I cooked up a jar full of sauce made 6 or 8 pies and 3 or 4 cakes and baked a whole boiler full of bread. Then he sent for the meat, a lot of beef to boil and a large roast. We had abundance of vegetables sweet and Irish potatoes, cabbage, carrots, onions, tomatoes, squash etc. much more than we could use and no sale for them. But the afternoon before they were to come it started to drizzle. The shed roof leaked and the ground floor was wet. I was working hard but got wet and [my] feet wet so that night I took a hard chill followed by a hot fever and such suffering as I had never known before. So John went for Mrs. Strohl and she worked over me all the rest of the night and when I was easier and she went home she forbade my getting up for 3 or 4 days under penalty of being worse than before.

The rain kept the threshers back one day so J.T. went and engaged the Widow Manzer to come and cook for them but she refused to try to do it alone so he got one of the Smith girls to help her. I felt pretty sore at having to hire 2 women to do the work after I had it nearly all done as the bread, pies, sauce and cake all lasted till after they were gone. But J.T. did not care if there were two women or a dozen. All he wanted was to see me get up again and sing around for I was always singing when well and he loved to hear me.

Mrs. Manzer brought her youngest child, Grace, along. She was about Willie's age but fatter and used to having her own way and of course Willie did not know how to play with other children so I wondered how they would get along. Grace found some pieces of broken dishes back of the sod house and had Willie help gather them up and take them to the well to wash and then they came to the house for something to wash them in. Mrs. Manzer gave them a dish and the dipper to dip some water from the tank. While there Willie came to my bed and said quite disdainfully "Mama Grace thinks those old broken dishes are good to play with." And I said to Mrs. Manzer "You see he is not used to playing with girls" and Willie I told to go on and help play her way and he would learn how and like it.

My bed was opposite the door and I could see out to the well where they were playing. They seemed to get along all right but suddenly as I looked Willie was bending over washing the dishes best he knew I suppose but probably he did not do it to suit Grace for I saw her hit him a hard crack with the dipper right on the back of his head. He straightened up gave a hard wink and then looked at her in great disgust. Then [he] marched with head up and shoulders thrown back to the house and up to my bedside and said "Ma I have been hit on the head with a dipper. And I ain't used to it, and I don't like it." Mrs. Manzer and I could not keep our faces straight but she hurried out to talk to Grace and I told Willie he needn't wash any more dishes as he could not do it to suit, so go and get his horses and play with them. So away he ran to get his horses, sticks with a strap nailed to one end for a halter, and the way those horses galloped and bucked around there for awhile was a caution.

The threshing being done, as J.T. hauled off the wheat he

brought back lumber enough to enclose a room 12 x 16 one story high with floor and shingle roof. But we could not spare enough money to finish it off with windows and lath and plaster so we knew we could not spend the winter in it. So they dug out a good cellar under it and put cellar windows in the south and [we] moved into it for the winter living mostly upstairs until real cold weather.

As Father needed John at home he debated with me whether he better go home where he knew he could not get along very well or run away to our Aunt's in Wisconsin and try and get a chance to go to school. We owed him a small wage for his work, for he would not take much as he considered it his home, but enough to more than buy his ticket to Madison. "If I only had a better suit of clothes" he said "or was sure some of them wanted me I would go." But though he felt sure someone in that country would have work [and] he could earn his way he was afraid his relatives might feel obliged to keep him whether they wanted to or not. So finally he said he would abandon the thought of more schooling and "try and be content to be an old bull whacker." So we traded him our R.R. eighty for what we owed him and he went home to Father's.

Fred we had not heard from though we had watched and waited in vain. Not a line even to let us know if he was alive.

Besides fixing the house J.T. had a lot of backsetting to do which is plowing the new breaking. John had helped him to put up quite a lot of hay as we had several head of cattle. The Railroad was building up the Republican River that year and we knew that freighting was at an end. But many movers stopped for hay so we put up a goodly supply.

A little while before Christmas J.T. went to Hastings among other businesses to see about disposing of our surplus young roosters. He took 28½ pounds and we sent 45 pounds soon after. We had eaten them all summer from as soon as they were large enough and still had quite a number to dispose of which were nice and plump. Fred Blake the butcher said if they were as nice as those he would pay us some more than regular market price. An old account book shows the price was 6 cents a pound which was considered good then. We had quite a time the day we dressed them but Father and John came over and we got them all ready for market before we went to bed and started for town with them early the next morning. These were really dressed ready to cook head feet feathers and entrails out. J.T. said that was my money ($9.36 for 156 pounds). I spent the most of it before we went home for cloth to make good warm clothes for us all saving some for garden seed and some farm papers.

When the weather was real cold but yet no snow so the roads were good, probably about January 1st, J.T. concluded he would take the team and haul up wood from the Blue which would be so much nicer than burning stalks or cow chips. So he took an early start and carried his dinner and supper. It must have been 15 miles or more but we thought with the horse team he could make it and cut a load of wood too. I did not look for him very early but a cold wind set in from the north and finally some snow with it so I knew he would be real cold when he got home so I set up and kept the house warm till he came and sure enough he was terrible chilled and had walked most of the way too facing that cold wind.

Well the amount of it was the next day he had a real fever and kept his bed and a real swelling come up on his forehead and grew fast till it closed one eye and looked very angry. I did not know what in the world to do and in the night he got so burning hot and commenced to talk wildly I concluded to go for Father.

I dreaded to go as on looking out I saw it was as black as I ever saw a night and I had never been over there but had heard J.T. say once that if you headed Frank and Bill east he was sure they would go to Juniata if south to Strohl's and if west over to Father's. I knew they had laid out a new road down across the draw northwest of King's but did not know within $\frac{1}{2}$ mile of where and too dark to see anyway. I did not know how to harness the team as I had never had occasion to try but thought if I got the harness on the collars and tugs fastened some way to the wagon it would have to go. I had the lantern to get hitched up and then went in the house to say good-by and J.T. seemed rational just then but insisted I must take the baby with me. I was terribly afraid to do that as I knew I might tip over on the draw but he insisted so I took her little cradle out and covered her over in it with a quilt. I knew she would not wake till I got back if I left her but to pacify him I had to take her.

Well I got in and put the lantern under the seat to have in an emergency. Why I did not hang it on the end of the tongue I don't know only I suppose I had never seen it done. I could not see the horses at all but when I judged we had got to the road I pulled the line to turn them west across the prairie. That night was one of the horrors of my life. Afraid of the horses anyway and afraid to try to guide them I could only hang on hope we would come out all right. While worried over my husband at home and the baby with me in case of an upset, it seemed we were travelling forever through a dark space.

Many times we went down a little ditch which I wondered if it was the draw and then we seemed to go straight down. I slid onto my feet and braced to deep from falling onto the horses, then a little level and some kind of a turn and I was sure they had left the road, then almost straight up which made them scratch to get the wagon up onto level ground. Now I knew that was the draw for sure but whether we had taken the right turn or not I had no way to learn.

Finally after what seemed hours the horses stopped and I dared not urge them on not knowing why they had stopped. But just as I started to climb down to find out I was overjoyed to hear Father's voice call out "Hallow, who's there?" I assured him I was and that J.T. was awful sick. "Well hold on a minute. I will come and show you the way in." And as he stepped out he exclaimed over the darkness and wondered how in the world I ever found the way. "I didn't, the horses did" I told him. So I had to go in and tell him all I could about what ailed J.T. and he got together some things he thought he might need for him.

When we started out he found lots of fault with my harnessing. I had the wrong harness on the right horse it seems so the lines were wrong and some of them not hitched. I told him I did not dare use the lines anyway. I think I had the collars on all wrong or else the harness but anyway we were there and he soon straightened things out. It had started to get a little light by the time we got to the draw and I shuddered to see where we had come down in the dark, and Father told me I was braver than he was which set me up considerable.

Father carried the cradle in and the baby never knew she had taken a night ride. Father said J.T. had erysipelas in his face which is what he had supposed from what I told him and he went to work bathing it with a solution of copper and did some other things and stayed awhile and in a day or two J.T. was around but he never went to the Blue for any more wood and I did not want him to. Father told J.T. to teach me how to harness a team before I broke my neck.

The spring of 1880 was dry and windy but we were glad to move up out of the cellar at first signs of warm weather and began making garden sometime in the last of February. Notwithstanding the fact that all the old neighbors had told me I would never be well again as I was broken down with hard work etc. I found myself enjoying good health as well as ever in my life.

J.T. went to Hastings one day and there was a sale of household furniture on the street. He bought an oldfashioned Boston rocker pretty well worn and it was a source of great joy and comfort to us all especially baby Susie and I. Many of my happiest hours have been spent holding a baby up tight and rocking it and I never can see that the ones who were rocked were inferior to those who were not but they certainly were more contented and happier.

He also saw a little rubber doll that day in a store where he went to purchase something I had sent for. It was the first one he had ever seen and would cry so comically when pressed or patted on the back he could not resist paying a quarter for it and bringing it home to Susie. Oh the good times she had hugging it up close like she liked to be held and rocking it in the old Boston rocker. He gave 60 cents for the chair and I am sure 85 cents never gave more comfort and pleasure.

Willie would eye the doll with great interest but seldom offered to touch it. In fact he had not much chance as she seldom let it out of her sight or arms and he evidently considered it was a girl's plaything anyway so he did not think it consistent with his dignity to handle it "before folks." But one day when Susie woke up her doll was missing and quite a search failed to find it at last.

"Willie do you know where Susie's doll is?"

"No."

"Have you seen it since she had it?"

"Yes."

"Did you have it?"

"Yes."

"What did you do with it?"

"Don't know."

"Did you take it outdoors?"

"Yes."

"Well go with me and show me where you went."

We started and at the corner of the house he paused.

"I had it here and squeaked it."

"Then where did you go?"

He went out by the chicken coop and said "I had it here and squeaked it."

"Then where did you go from here?"

"I went to the windmill platform" he said. "I sat down here and squeaked it."

So back and forth to the barn and corn crib he had been and squeaked it. Following up the path he had gone one step at a time [until] at last he came to the Marsh harvester.

"I stood right here and squeaked it."

"Then where?"

"I don't know. You called me and I went to the house."

But I could see the doll where he had laid it when I called him on the bundle carrier which was a little above his head where he could not see it and he had doubtless laid it down so I would not see him playing with a doll. I have found that the way with children. Mostly they can only remember one step at a time and few do things to be naughty until they have been taught by older people.

We had bought a windmill on time of course that spring as we had considerable stock and J.T. had not time to draw so much water and so many other chores and do the field work too and I never was very good at drawing water with a windlass. Susie would sit and watch the wheel go around with never ending delight and wonder and I certainly enjoyed having plenty of fresh water and some for the garden as well.

There were a good many movers going west into the western counties that spring as there had been for a year or two. In fact some days there were movers' wagons in sight most of the time and with the windmill even more than the usual number stopped for water. One of the outfits had 2 or 3 covered wagons and a regular little house built on a wagon and a good sized bunch of cattle along. I was out by the well when they came for water and they had left their wagons by the road where they camped for dinner first asking J. T. for permission I suppose.

There was an old man and some sons and the old man said his wife would like to have me come and see her house as she was proud of it. And no wonder for she was travelling in comfort if one ever did in those days. She said they came out to Iowa when it was new and they were young and went through all kinds of hardships and now when they had everything comfortable their sons and their wives all wanted to go west and get cheap land and their father got the fever too just as bad and wanted to go with his boys. "But" she said "I put my foot right down and said after so many years' hard work we have got so we can be comfortable at last and I am not going to another new country and go through it all over again." But the boys said "Ma if you will go we will build you a house on a wagon so you will be comfortable on the road and you can live in it till we get you a comfortable house built." "So" she said "here we are." She had a bed across the front end and a window in the front. Her husband sat on a seat outside part of the time and part inside and drove through the window. There was a window on both sides so she could see the country and be out of the dust and wind or have them open in nice weather, and a door and steps behind [and] a little table on one side and a rocking chair and work basket and a closet in one corner with some clothes hung up out of the dust.

They have something like that on auto[s] nowdays but I never saw one I liked as well as that. Many of those who went west that spring came back that fall or the next. Some stayed till '94 or '5 or '6 if they had money enough but most of them who tried to farm came back, but I never saw them again.

But however discouraged the older people were when they came back the children were happy. I remember well some children who went by singing, "We are going back east, we are going back east, to stay with Grandpa." Lucky those who had a grandpa or as the men used to say, "Going back to see my wife's folks." There are thousands of old abandoned wells fallen in out in Hayes, Chase, Perkins and other western counties dug by those who had to go back and "visit their wife's folks."

Before harvest as we had quite a harvest of our own and our harvester was not much good and J.T. found he could get all the wheat he could cut if he got a header we all went to town and I got some things for harvest and we brought home an 8 foot Randolph header which was one of the best buys we ever made. We made quite a holiday of it. I took a little lunch with us and we bought some crackers and cheese which always seemed to us a great treat and coming home Willie and Susie sat awhile in the elevator of the header which was loaded in the wagon and we sang songs and were very young and hopeful and jolly. Life looked good to us then and we often planned of the large family we would have and the many additions we would build on the house as we needed them. Of how we would have a real home and raise all the fruit and everything we needed. And we planned or I did to have things as much like Grandpa Sanford's place was when I was a little girl as we could. And they always had a cellar full of everything good to eat with abundance of the best butter and cheese and fresh fruit of every description. It seemed to us it would be wicked to raise a family and not do our best to provide all those things for them so to that end we set out all the things we could afford to get to make our home homelike.

Aunt Hattie gave me some Lilac bushes she had brought from Grandpa's old home and young gooseberries and currant bushes as well as strawberries. I think I told you of our terrible disappointment when our strawberries blossomed. "Liar blossoms" Willie called them and [they] did not bear any not a single berry though hers bore full. But we had taken the most vigorous looking plants and they were all pistillate. Grandfather Smith had taught me a good deal about gardening but more about fruit growing and of course J.T. only knew about fruit as it came on the table but we took some farm papers and tried to learn all we could. Most of the neighbors would only say "Oh you can't raise fruit here," "The wind would blow it all off if you did," "It would blow the gooseberries off a gooseberry bush" etc. So we had to do the best we could.

Aunt Sophy had sent me $1.00 the spring Jimmie was a baby [and] said to get something for the children with it. While we were studying what best to get a fruit tree pedlar came along and we bought 2 apple trees for 50 cents apiece. They were tall slim things I would not take as a gift now but we thought they were fine and that the children would soon be able to eat some real apples. We looked up in our papers to see the best way to set them and it said dig a hole 4 feet square and put the topsoil in the bottom etc. So J.T. took his square and dug two holes just exactly 4 feet square and 4 feet deep and we set them out with great satisfaction and high hopes.

We put the top dirt in the bottom [and] straightened each root exactly so and watered it well as we went along. We were mighty proud of the job but alas. Jimmie's only leaved out very fully and died about the time he did. We would dig a hole by Willie's and water it well [and] often but it never made much growth and died in a few years.

But now in 1880 another tree pedlar came along and we bought 100 strawberry plants and 50 grape vines from him and as J.T. was so busy I got Lansing Cline to help me set them and we sure did a good job. J.T. had the ground as fine as it could be worked and we planned a strawberry bed clear to the road and 2 rows of grapes the same. This was before we got the windmill and it was a very windy miserable day. We set the strawberries but we put each one on a little mound of fine dirt according to the book and spread out every root just so and lugged abundance of water and wet each one and then drew dry dirt over each one. The fact that the roots were all dark colored did not signify anything to us [as] the book had not said anything about that.

A young man came along looking for work who said he had worked in orchards in Iowa so J.T. had him stay a day or two and help me set the grapes as we would not trust anyone not interested to set them alone. We had heeled the grapes in at once according to directions and let them stay till he got most of the holes dug. He dug large holes as I told him and carried rotten manure and put [it] in the bottom and covered it with topsoil and now for the grape vines. When he saw them he gasped "But these won't grow. These are dead." "What makes you think so?" we asked. "Oh can't you see the roots are little and black and live vine will look more yellow." But we were sure the man we got them of looked like a nice man who would not sell us dead things so we had him go ahead and set them.

But often when I turned around and he would be sifting the dry dirt among the roots according to the book he would be smiling and once he laughed right out when was watering them and said "I never took so much pains over with a live vine before let alone a dead one." And he was right for neither strawberry or grape ever showed a leaf. But that did not keep me from carrying water to them until we got the mill for we still hoped.

J. T. struck a congenial calling when it came to driving a header and Frank and Bill did also. Almost right away they learnt how to swing out as he rounded the corners and did not need the lines. All he had to do was tend to the tiller wheel and the other team. Frank and Bill were great walkers and the header ran light. J. T. would measure off a field exact to a foot and cut up the middle and down through the middle of each side the first thing and have a place for the stacks in the center. Then he always had 3 header boxes and kept them busy. He got a good crew who did not keep him waiting and would cut according to the size of the field 30 to 35 or 40 acres in a day. Once cutting for Boody he had just got a 50 acre field started one night and finished it about 45 acres the next day. He got 50 cents an acre for cutting and furnished both teams or 40 cents and the owner furnished one team. He cut 400 acres the first year.

There are not many days when I do not see the picture in memories hall of J. T. standing on the header with his white shirt gray trousers and wide felt hat. I was mighty proud of him and have never seen before or since such a handsome real man's man. He had always worn white shirts as a bridge foreman and I could not bear to see him in any others in the summer so always made them of unbleached muslin with linen cuffs and collars and the gray trousers I made as Grandma Smith who had learned the tailor trade taught me. And they always fit so nice and he could not bear to (and I could not have him) so he did not wear overalls for years.

Nor did he wear dirty shirts. In all the warm weather he always took off his shirt at night bathed the sweat off put on a night shirt and always had a clean white shirt for morning. The cloth only cost 10 cent a yard and I traded eggs for it and always got several at a time he could look nice and they washed easy as I could boil them. Many old ladies have told me how nice they always remembered him with his white shirts. But for winter he had dark blue flannel shirts which were warm and looked nice too.

Having lost Jimmie we were naturally very anxious about baby Susie and we had heard or someone told us that if we kept her well until September 1st all danger would be over. So on the morning of September 1st J.T. woke me. He had been playing with baby and he said "Wake up mama it is September 1st and we have our baby well." She was then 1 year and 2 days old a dainty little thing with only 2 little teeth but never sick only in the spring.

But the babies had been dying around us that summer with Cholera Infection so-called. John Ellis lost their baby and Sam Higgins their 2 little ones right on our section and as I had been afraid of contagion so had hardly been away from home. In a few days Susie began to sicken a little. We thought it was her teeth and someone had been there with whooping cough so we thought she would have it. J.T. said we must never let a doctor tell us again it is too late. I will let the plowing go and we will take her down to see her Doctor Gilman. So it was. I put up some lunch and we made a holiday of it. Susie sat on the seat between us when not on her father's lap and whenever she saw pretty flowers on the prairie she would stretch out her hand for them and J.T. would stop and jump out and get them. I suppose she thought it quite a game for she kept it up till we had quite a load of flowers but J.T. did not tire as long as she wanted more. We got a little more lunch at Snowflake P.O. and drove on to the doctor's not far from there.

Susie was glad to see him and he her and they had quite a time together and he did not say it was too late or look worried so we were greatly relieved. The doctor's wife was a fine sweet-faced old lady, made me think of Grandma Smith. We visited a little and the doctor having given us some medicine with full directions, give this if so and if so do that, for it was a long way to come, we went home greatly relieved.

But she did not get better. Her gums were so swollen we thought that was it and she coughed considerable, still not bad as many so we kept anxious hearts and [were] doing the best we knew. First we would think she was better and then afraid not. Father came over and advised with us and we hoped all would be well till suddenly she went into a convulsion. We put her into hot water [and] sent for Father and Dr. Gilman but before morning she died.

The doctor did not get there until light. I had her washed and laid out but could not bear to entirely close her little blue eyes. And when he came in and saw her he cried "Oh my baby my baby" and with tears rolling down his cheeks he said "Her bright eyes, her pretty blue eyes, they are brighter in death than most are alive."

Then he told us his wife knew more than he did, that as soon as we were gone that day she had said that he must not be so taken up with the baby for he would have to give her up. "Why" he told her "she is not bad and I am sure they will take good care of her."

"Yes" she said "they will and you will do all you can do but no use. She will not live. She is too spiritual and her body is not strong enough to stand the combination of teething bowel trouble and whooping cough." But he said though he had great respect for her opinion he felt sure she was mistaken; but she was right.

We had been so disgusted when Jimmie died at the swarm of strangers who overran the house and grounds in more curiosity than sympathy it seemed to me that we felt we could not endure another such trial especially with our house in its unfinished shape. So father drove to Juniata for the coffin saying nothing to anyone except O.H. Wright who promised to say nothing to anyone, only to send and let Aunt Hattie and Uncle Chester know. And J.T. went down to Strohls and told them but for them not to tell anyone. They said all right but Mrs. Strohl asked who would be there and sent word for me not to worry about any dinner.

The funeral was to be at 2 o'clock. About 10 or eleven

Wrights and Uncle Clewett and Aunt Hattie came and I was out at the windmill when they drove up. I felt just stunned as if the bottom had fell out of my life and the world. But I did not seem to want to cry or make a fuss. Aunt Hattie came and put her arms around me while her tears ran fast. She said "The only comfort I can see is she will never have to suffer as you do now."

And really that did help. I realized our grief had been too selfish. We thought too much of our home left desolate and not about her side. How oft in later years we used to say "We have lost all the babies, but two, Jimmie and Susie, are always babies to us, their cute little baby ways always as dear and plain as if it were yesterday." Aunt Hattie said "We will start a little fire and Aunt (Mrs. Wright) and I will fix a little dinner" but I told her Mrs. Strohl sent word not to do anything about eating. "Well" she said "she must be going to bring something but had we not best make some coffee or something warm to go with it."

Just then someone said Strohls were coming so they waited and I never shall forget. She had a big coffee boiler full of coffee, some roast chicken, mashed potatoes, sweet potatoes, cold slaw, pie and everything ready to put on the table. The dishes of potatoes etc. had been placed in a tub with the hot coffee in the center and all covered tight. She had brought a tablecloth knowing baby had been sick [and] I might not have washed, and as quietly as any undertaker the dinner was placed on the table and I really did eat some for I had been too anxious to eat for some days. The dishes were quietly placed back in the tub (some things left were placed in my pantry) and the place looked as if no meal had taken place there.

The bible was placed on the table. Aunt Hattie and some of them sang. Uncle Chester prayed. O.H. Wright read the scripture and made some good remarks and we went out and laid our Susie by our little boy.

I cannot describe the terrible days that followed. For the first time we felt discouraged about our large family. I felt that we could not endure to lose any more. In fact I think my brain was so numbed nothing seemed normal. Willie teased me to play with him and I would put him off that I was busy or had not time till one day he burst out "I don't care. I think it was mean of you to get big before I did so you can't play." That helped me to realize again my selfishness for I just wanted to nurse my grief.

I had a constant and terrible headache and my hair was very long and extremely heavy so I thought it would relieve me to have it cut off. J.T. thought so too and as of course no one ever thought of going to a barber. I wanted him to cut it and several times he got the shears but he would lift up my hair and say "I can't do it." So one day when the pain seemed unbearable I took the shears and cut out a chunk and then took them out where he was plowing. He said "How could you?" and some other things but he cut the rest of it but it did not do any good. Cutting hair will not cure a broken heart.

Finally J.T. had me take Willie [and] go over to Aunt Hattie's and stay a day while he plastered the lean-to with clay so we could have it for a comfortable kitchen, and we put our bed in the pantry as we could not afford to plaster the whole of the house, so the change helped even if only for a day. I got a little boy's waist pattern from her and came home and made Willie some pretty waists and so began to take more interest in life again.

We had a very long and cold winter set in early and had lots of snow. The draws between our place and Father's were all drifted level full of snow. There was so much snow around the house and yard that J.T. mostly tended the chickens for about the first time and Willie and I housed up pretty close not having overshoes or things suitable for the heavy snow. Without the kitten I hardly know how Willie could have gotten through this lonesome period shut in by the walls of an 8 x 12 containing stove table and sewing machine.

J.T. had bought me a new Singer machine and I made good use of it making all the clothes we all wore. I had done this before by hand only occasionally taking some long seams down to sew on Mrs. Strohl's machine. Machines were not so high then. I think we paid 30 or 35 dollars for it. I would move the table to the center of the room and Willie would tie a little piece of corn cob on to a string and run around and around the table with the kitten chasing the cob. They would keep this up by the hour and it got very tiresome to me but I realized that they needed the exercise.

When spring finally came we could not get up the usual

enthusiasm about planting etc. We were sorely oppressed yet with our grief and fully decided that if we were ever to have any more children we would not allow ourselves to love them so well. We had been brought up to the Calvinistic idea of a jealous God and felt we might have merited punishment as we had certainly thought more of our babies than of God.

I had taken much pride in the fact that the garden and chickens with milk from 2 cows and a couple pigs to butcher had not only made our living but bought our groceries and clothing as well. It was my joy to think that everything J.T. made could go into needed equipment to farm better and more as more land was broke up for farming. And as work is never drudgery for those we love so it had been a delight to me to have the best and largest garden the best and the largest flock of chickens and so be able to have the pleasure of setting as good a table as could be found.

But this Spring J.T. felt dissatisfied that the price of crops never seemed to be enough to pay necessary expenses. This made me also blue but I strove to make him believe that times would surely be better when we had got a better start and so we both tried to work harder and spend less but it now began to seem as if work as we might we were not getting ahead as we ought, certainly not as we had hoped, or expected.

It was customary in those days to have a summer and winter term of school. The State helped pay for this from the rent of school lands, 2 sections of land in each township having been set apart for school purposes. As teachers only received about 20 per month the state in our district paid for about 3 months' school a year and in order to keep taxes down many of the voters who had no particular interest in the school used to try to limit the school to 3 months. Women had no voice whatever in school affairs (or any other) so of course never attended the meetings but J.T. always went and voted for as much school as he could get anyone else to support [with] him and thereby incurred some enmity among the Bendys and others who were our wealthiest citizens but had no children of school age.

This spring Willie started to school. I went with him the first day and so did the yellow kitten, now a cat, [which] followed along about a mile. He had a mile and a half to go to where the old Mayflower schoolhouse used to stand. I got a very amusing account of his first day from the teacher afterwards. Of course I had told him to be a good boy and study his lesson but it seemed he did not understand the meaning of the word study. The teacher found he knew his letters and how to count and assigned him a lesson in the first reader, short words about a boy and dog with a picture of it. He watched and saw the rest of the scholars looking steadily at their books and then the teacher would have them come and recite it. He looked on his book and pondered all of the things that boy could do with the dog. So when she called him he went up without hesitation and recited a long list of adventures off very glibly none of which of course had any relation to the book. Poor boy he was doing the best he could but the children snickered and even the teacher could not keep from smiling as he went on and on till she halted him finally and read the lesson over to him. She told me it was the funniest thing she ever saw in her life to see him go on and on in the same tone of voice the others recited in just as if he was reading a lot of stuff which no one ever heard of before. After that I often went a piece with him in the morning, sometimes a mile, but yellow pussy always went the mile and then came back alone.

We had a wonderful garden this year planting everything in long rows so J.T. could cultivate with a hoe. We raised about everything in the seed catalogue that would grow in this climate and in the greatest abundance. I have not the figures in poultry for that year but for the year before I sold 344 pounds of dressed chicken at 5 and 6 cents a pound, sold and used 71 at about 25 cents a piece, used and sold 257 dozen eggs at an average of less than 10 cents a dozen, and carried over about 120 young pure-blood Brahma hens so that during this year we had by more eggs etc. than ever before.

In fact, our place became quite noted for its "white" chickens that were all "just alike" but Willie and I knew most of them apart and many of them by name. J.T. liked the chickens but did not like to feel that he owed me for his living so it was his notion that I keep account of expenses and income and he had given me 2 cows Lady and Topsy to pay for what we used in 1879 and 1880.

But the year wore on and come fall we had a fine crop of wheat and to save as much time as possible I hauled several loads of wheat while a hired man helped J.T. put up the frame, and the horses were otherwise idle and brought back loads of lumber both shingles etc. for we were going to lath and plaster the 12 x 16 room. And to this end Father and Strohl had come up one day and helped J.T. raise the roof 4 feet so we could floor it and have a bedroom for extra and also for Willie upstairs. This then made a lot extra work but we had always been so crowded for room that many things had spoiled for lack of protection from storm and wind. One of the last of the trips I made to Kenesaw with wheat was against a very strong north wind which though not cold was very tiring and unpleasant. I drove to the elevator where a Scotch friend of J.T., Mr. Lindsay, called a man to take the team and unload it while I took some eggs over to the store to trade for groceries.

Soon coming back I found team and grain check ready and went to Cooley's lumber yard and gave them the bill of lumber J.T. had sent for which was duly loaded and I started for home. As I had left right after dinner I had to be back early as possible to get supper. The wind had grown still stronger but I flattered myself that as soon as we turned south it would be in the back so better.

I had a very heavy comforter along which was on the seat and over the back and a lot of it lying on the lumber behind the seat. It was a tall load of lumber but I felt no fear for was used to driving Frank and Bill by that time. But just as we turned the corner to go south the wind seemed to get a new hold and turned the heavy comforter completely over my head and arms and rolled me quick as a flash off the seat and down between the team and the load. I never was so surprised for it was done quick as a flash but I said and remember that I controlled my voice and spoke coolly "Whoa Bill" for I realized it was him I would hit. And he stopped, never moved another foot. Frank took one step but Bill stood as if rooted while I untangled myself from the quilt and finally managed to roll out and then pull out the quilt and finally get the lines straightened out. I had quite a job to get the heavy quilt back on the load as both sides of it were covered with denim made [on] purpose to keep out the cold and wind [while] riding as we had no robe. But I folded it and never left a loose end of quilt to blow around in the wind again.

I was not hurt but felt kind of shaky yet when I got home and though I am not sure I think that was the last load for me that fall. Old Man Higgins came and plastered the house for us and I will always remember how he would stop and sing a little to hear how fine it sounded in the empty room and I enjoyed it too in spite of all the dirt the plastering made. Then J.T. wainscoted it and put a double window in the south and my I felt proud and happy so J.T. was happy to see me so.

Right away then Frank Burns, their oldest boy, got sick and died and his dog Jack ran way and came over to stay with us. Seemed he could not stand it there without Frank. He was a fine shephard dog and we wanted to be good to him but they said for us not to feed him so he would come home. He was only there a day or so when I got sick in the night and J.T. went for Mrs. Manzer again.

I suppose Jack thought the getting up in the night etc. was like the sickness at home for all the time J.T. was gone he lay under my window and howled the most mournful howl I ever heard. Lucky I was not superstitious but still I certainly did not enjoy his doleful noise and tried to drive him away but only seemed to make him worse.

Well before morning Jessie was born on October 30, celebrating the Scotch Halloween you see. She was larger than Jimmie or Susie and real plump, weighed 9 or 9½ pounds [with a] perfect large chest which showed large lungs and all vital organs and we had resolved not to love her. Well my resolution got very weak as soon as I took her in my arms but I did not say anything and J.T. who always hung around the new baby did not say much for awhile [and] then he burst out "God help us mother we can't help ourselves. She is going to be just as dear as the others." And so she was and always was much the dearer as our hearts were so tender and distressed.

Healthy and happy she was a blessing to us from the first minute the entire 20 years she stayed with us. Her father and Willie had an added attraction in the house and I was able to resume my singing, something I always did unconsciously unless too unhappy. This pleased J.T. who always loved to hear it as he knew then I was happy.

During these years we had not heard from brother Fred though we were very anxious about him and John confessed he was like me and never saw a stranger coming either afoot or horseback without hoping it might possibly be Fred. Father was down to Lincoln on business either buying or selling sheep that fall and met a man who told him where Fred had been working. And one night when Jessie was about a month old we were preparing for bed when a knock came. J.T. went to the door and in a minute exclaimed "Fred where did you come from?" Of course, I hurried out and it was really Fred grown to a tall young man but [with] the same dark eyes and dimpled cheek he had as a baby.

There was not much sleep that night and in the morning. After telling us of his many adventure he went over to Father's to see him and John so there was another happy meeting.

Fred went right to work for Father with John shucking corn feeding sheep and hogs etc. etc. They had lots of work to do always. Putting up barrels of Kraut to sell in Hastings digging and marketing sweet potatoes etc. etc.

That winter a Farmers' Alliance was organized at the schoolhouse by W. A. McKeighan. I was not there and think I only attended once when J.T. was to read a piece he had been assigned on preparing ground for a crop of spring wheat. I was interested in that of course and copied it in a scrapbook which I still have and a very good piece it is. The reason he was given the subject was that we had been having the best crops of spring wheat in the country.

The Alliance at this time was not supposed to be political but I cannot but surmise that McKeighan knew that if the farmers once got organized and discussing their situation they would eventually find they had to resort to politics to get any needed reform. However politics was the furthest thing from my mind then. I had always been raised a strict republican and taught that by freeing the slaves and saving the nation that [Lincoln?] had done a wonderful and God-led work in spite of the wicked democrats. J.T. was always somewhat amused by my stand but we never let any of those things disturb our domestic life for we loved one another too dearly to openly disagree or discuss points on which we were not agreed. So we slipped through a very happy winter again. We had a double window in the south end of our sitting room and I kept Jessie there lying in the sun whenever it shone and we did not have her up in our arms. And every Sunday the boys John and Fred came over for dinner and brought news and joy and laughter for all.

And J.T. made a wind plow which would run around the yard and pull a weight and was very amusing to the boys and everyone who came along. He always contended it was a shame to make the poor brutes work so hard to do our work when all we needed was to harness the wind of which we always had a surplus to do. He looked up about getting a patent for it and made a fine model but it seemed it would cost more than we could afford and he put it off and nothing came of it. Horse flesh and ox flesh was so cheap we feared folks would not use it as it would take a rope or wire as long as the field but it would be much cheaper and better than the tractor I believe.

As spring opened and I got busy running between chicken coop and house, garden and house, well and house etc. etc. Jessie having gotten large enough so she was liable to kick out of the rocking chair we placed her in a cracker box with a little pillow in the bottom and a quilt around the top and sides to soften them and a little sack of loose feathers over her feet to keep them warm. I felt perfectly safe to leave her for the few minutes at a time that I needed to and in case of being out long I would take her, box and all, along.

One noon Willie brought the cattle in at noon for a drink for though only 6 years old he was herding them and a good herder he was too. He ate his dinner and as J.T. was gone for the day, although I was very busy washing which was always hard for me, I went out to help him get them out of the corral and out to the stacks he was herding them around. I set Jessie in her box by the east window where she could see the corral and us as we brought the cattle near the house and she sat there as we went by and smiled at us and waved her little hand.

I expected to go clear to the stack with him but something seemed to call me back. I was sure baby was all right still [it] seemed as if I must go. So telling Willie to go on I turned around and run and the further I ran the more it seemed I must hurry so ran fast as I could. As I neared the house realized she was not crying but when I opened the door and stepped in I saw her lying forward with her little face in the loose feather pillow and big drops of sweat on the back side of her head like a chicken that is smothered in the shell. I suppose she threw herself forward trying to see more of us and was not strong enough to raise herself up again and the nice little warm pillow I thought was so fine for her came up all around her little face and smothered her. I grabbed her up and blew in her mouth and took her to the tub of rinse water and threw some in her face with no result.

Words cannot describe my feelings. These were not days of near neighbors or telephones. And my baby was to all appearance dead. Desperately I ran to the door with her in my arms to see if possibly anyone was in sight on the road. No one was but there was a terrible wind, one of the very hardest which as I gazed around seemed to blow right into her lungs and she gave a slight gasp, just one a little one but enough to show there was some life. So back to the tub of water I ran and threw some in her face and this time there was a slight quiver. Back to the open door again and another gasp. It seemed as if the wind would take away what breath I had so did not dare keep her there long. So back and forth I went and blew in her mouth and everything I could think of in my distraction. A bit of camphor under her nose seemed to help till finally she opened her eyes and began to breathe more regular. And no words can ever portray the relief and joy I felt. How glad how wonderfully rejoiced I was that J.T. did not have to return to a house of mourning. After that no more nice little soft pillow around a baby for me.

The McKays, some kind of a cousin to Strohls, lived on a homestead cornering the section of Father's timber claim. Mrs. McKay was state agent for some corset company and she and her daughter Grace were away on that business a great deal. He had been a large merchant in the east in Boston I think and had a bad failure which he never got over so as to be able to transact much business and they moved west without much means and as she declared herself the head of the family, as she was, the homestead was taken in her name. She then carried on the corset business and got money enough to get the place broke out and keep things running and the boys Ed and Fred, Tim and Guy, with the father batched and ran a herd of cattle on sand creek. We had our cattle in their herd several summers and used to drive down occasionally to see how they thrived, and the boys especially Fred had worked for us in harvest, threshing, etc. so we felt pretty well acquainted.

The boys told their mother about my nice chickens and she came over to see them and wanted to buy some so I sold her 12 young thoroughbred Brahma hens and a rooster for $1.00 each and felt pretty proud with my 13 dollars in cash. And as the boys found out I wanted to go to town to spend it John came over in a new Studebaker spring wagon Father had bought and a little team of mules Jack and Jill and took me to Juniata.

I went first to the furniture store as I had made up my mind to try and get a baby carriage for Jessie and have a better place to keep her. Though I had never seen one since I came to the state I knew I wanted one. The furniture man told me his wife was talking of selling hers as their baby was too big to need it and I went to see it. It seemed very nice to me, almost as good as new every way and when she said she would take $5.00 for it I handed over the money at once and went back to the furniture store and bought a nice new red high chair with a shelf for $1.75. What I did with the rest of the money I have not the slightest idea but think I took it home and probably spent some of it for papers for we now took several papers and our eggs brought us all we needed of clothes and groceries. All we needed I say for as we never went where fine clothes were needed new calico and gingham was all we cared for and it was fairly cheap.

That day with John will be remembered as long as any particle of memory lasts as one of the bright ones of life. It was a great thing for him to have a holiday probably the first one since he had left us and we made the most of it. As we rode over the prairie cross lot most of the way we told stories and sang songs and had as good a time as anyone in a limousine can have. For we dearly loved each other and a cross word had never passed between us.

Jack was a sturdy heavy set little mule and Jill was slimmer and willing to go. And John always hit at Jill with the black snake to make them go and then she would hurry and Jack would hurry to keep up. I thought that was not fair though I could see he did not hurt the mule, more a loud snap of the whip than anything but I expostulated with him and he laughed and said "You always want to hit the mule that will go, no use to hit the other." And sure enough he showed he could snap the whip at Jack or even hit him real hard and he would not move a bit faster but when Jill hurried up he would hurry to keep up with her. So we had a good deal of fun all day and little knew I that it was my last visit with dear brother John.

For things were very unpleasant for the boys at home. Their stepmother made life a burden too hard to bear and Fred being now 21 wanted to go west and take up land of his own so as soon as the grass on the prairie was good enough to feed their mules at night they started, for Father let John go with Fred knowing it [was] much better for them to be together and feeling John had stood as much as he was called to. So he gave them each a little team of mules and a light wagon a little feed and his best wishes and I cooked them up a trunk full of grub. We had an old trunk with a raised top which would stand considerable rain without injuring the contents.

I baked a large pan of pork and beans roasted a couple of hens with dressing made a large fruit cake and a lot of bread and packed a lot of butter and sauce and pork and salt matches eggs and all and filled the trunk and more. When the boys came to say good-by and saw what I [had] done they were astonished and Fred declared "Lou we cannot take all that. We do not need it, we can never eat it all, it will spoil. We will not be clear out of the world. Here, unpack most of that stuff and we will buy what we want as we go along."

But John saw I was going to feel hurt and he always looked ahead and said "Oh you bet we will eat it all and glad to get it. My we will have a feast all the way and save our money. We can use all the money we have or are like to get." And indeed I do not know how much they had but probably not over 10 dollars.

So they loaded the trunk in, Fred still protesting a little that I ought not [have] gone to so much work and I let them go quite happily for the last thing John whispered to me "Lou I will always write to you [all] along if only a card for I know how we have worried over Fred so if you don't hear from me you may know I am dead." Oh John the best brother a girl ever had. Could I have known I would never see you again I would not could not let you go.

In course of time a letter came from them both and Fred wrote "Lou your lunch came in pretty handy as [we] were 5 days in the sand hills without seeing a house." How glad I have always been I did what I could.

As I was so well stocked with young hens I did not try to raise so many chickens and did less garden work that year and devoted my time more to the baby which did not do her any good as I know of, only spoil her a little bit. I wanted to be sure of all the time I needed for her 2 baths daily and more in the hot weather and making her the prettiest little clothes of any baby in the country. J.T. was anxious for me to be as well as possible while nursing the baby so said we must hire the washing done most of the time at least. So I got the Widow Manzer to come a day in the week to help and as I nearly always paid her the 50 cents (which was the highest wage given to women then) in butter or eggs chickens or garden truck we were not out much money and she was very glad to come especially as she often had buttermilk or various things to take home extra.

School meetings came on this year without much thought from me till one day Mrs. Manzer said "I wish Mr. Kellie would vote for as much winter school as we can get as my boys are getting so big now they will not go much more and all the Boody outfit are trying to get the school cut down to just the 3 months we are obliged to have to get the state apportionment. They none of them have any children but a number of their boys are old enough to vote and even the hired man who will not be here over 30 days is to be kept to vote their way."

Well that started me thinking. Her husband had died when the youngest was in long dresses leaving her with 8 children 4 boys and 4 girls. It would never be possible for them to go anywhere but to our district school and now for 4 years we had not had much school and of that in the summer when teachers were cheap and her big boys could not go. And she had no vote and no one to represent her as most of her best friends were in another school district. Right then I saw for the first time that a woman might be interested in politics and want nay need a vote. I had been taught it was unwomanly to concern oneself with politics and that only the worst class of woman would ever vote if they had a chance etc. etc. but now I saw where a decent mother might wish very much to vote on local affairs at least.

Of course J. T. promised to do all he could. I guess they had quite a row but he knew how to influence men and carried the day and started agitating for women's right to vote at school meetings. I don't know how much he helped but he sure worked for it and Father did the same. It was discussed in the Alliance and in a short time a woman if mother of a child of school age or a woman over 21 years of age who *paid taxes* could vote at the school election. Meanwhile any hired man over 21 who had been 30 days in the district could vote without any question of taxes. An improvement [but] still not just.

Seeing I had gotten interested in one small part of politics your father tried to interest me still further. "Why, if Mrs. Manzer for instance was interested in her children's school welfare should she not be equally so in having a clean community for them to grow up in? Why not be allowed for instance to vote against the saloon and in favor of clean men to enforce such local option laws as we had and to see that the saloons abided by the law etc.etc. You know she lives 1½ miles north from the school house and the last mile has never been worked at all and is very bad for the children to get over at times and between there and town the first mile is almost impassible lots of times with more that ½ a load of wheat. As she has no vote for road supervisor and no near neighbor who has, all the road work is being done north south and east of them where votes can be influenced."

These and other arguments of his had a good deal of influence with me but I still objected that no good woman would or could go to the polls to vote in that drunken, fighting, smoking outfit. Not fit for a woman to be in the town election day or night, say nothing about going near the polls. Of course it was different in our little school elections where all were neighbors but in that drunken rowdy element, never.

For as far back as I could remember in Wisconsin in [the]

time of the civil war I could remember drunken men going by whipping their horses and swearing as they never did any other day. And we children were not allowed to go downtown that day as there were so much danger of fights and drunken men driving teams and having runaways etc. But J.T. said the first thing of course had to be to clean up the polls and make it fit for any good woman to go to. In fact until that was done there was very little use of thinking of any other reform. [He said] "That will be the first thing the Farmers' Alliance will have to tend to and we will have the help of labor organizations in the cities so there is hope it will be done soon. Of course the way it is with every office seeker sending free liquor and cigars to every polling place it is not a decent place for any clean man let alone a woman. You know I hate a drunken outfit as bad as you do [and] so does your father and Uncle Chester and O.H. and many others. The trouble has been they have all kept fighting the war over and over and not taking up the new issues."

"Oh I suppose" I said "the democrats would send free liquor but I don't see why the republicans allow it."

"There is just as much yes more republican whiskey furnished at the polls as any other. Nearly all their candidates are represented by parties who furnish both tickets and booze and go with their men and see them deposit the ticket in the boxes. Many of our young men get their first taste of liquor and first cigars then." [missing text] "That is the worst thing there is" continued J.T. "While I always vote the prohibition ticket when there is one and try to vote for clean men they always wink on peddling liquor on election day."

"Well" I said "you will have to clean it up before you can ask or expect a woman to vote."

"We sure will" he declared. This was only a sample of many of our good natured talks.

To go back a little, this spring J.T. had prepared the ground for a large field of spring wheat. In accord with the paper he had read at the Alliance meeting he had harrowed it as for a garden until there was no part of it but was fit for onions or the finest seed. Of course he walked for all of this as riding harrows were unknown and he would not have ridden anyway as we were short of horse flesh. And he did not mind walking in those days.

After following the old A[?] harrow all day he would come in at night and I would ask "Tired?"

"Well" he would say "I don't mind anything only the great strain on the mind."

And often he would show me his shins black and blue where while he studied some problem for the betterment of the farmers and mankind he had forgotten and walked up and skinned his shins on the harrow, and he had to walk fast to do it as Frank and Bill were the fastest walkers in the country. He had trained them to walk fast but seldom allowed them to trot. I could always calculate just when he would be back if he went to Hastings or anywhere else. Whether with a load or not the team would walk 5 miles an hour and I knew just about how long he would let them rest. So they walked the same with the harrow. Still, even on that soft ground he nearly always kept his shins black and blue when harrowing.

He had heard that the Abrams[es] living several miles west of us had a new kind of wheat yielding much more than the kinds now being grown around us and they were selling for seed at some advance over the regular price for wheat. Abrams had moved from New York to Liberty Township Kearney County in 1879 with considerable money so they were considered wealthy. Anyway they seemed to have money to invest in anything they needed or wanted and they had sent and gotten this new wheat at considerable expense and had such a good crop they they were selling a lot of it to farmers for seed. J.T. decided to sell the wheat he had kept for seed and invest in the new kind. So it was done and he wanted me to go with him in the lumber wagon after the seed. So I packed us a lunch and we set out and it was quite an outing for me as it was very seldom I left the place.

We had a pleasant ride and Mr. Abrams came out and insisted on my going to the house with the baby. [He] said Mother and the girls would want to see it and soon some of them came out and insisted on my going in. I had imagined I would sit and wait while J.T. loaded up and we would start back and eat our lunch on the road. I had never been over in that part of the country before and was surprised at the many comforts that [they] had around them and the coolness of their large house.

The women folks all made a great fuss over the baby. While I had imagined they would be stuck up and cool they were very cordial insisting on my taking off my things [and] that it would not be a great while after he got loaded up till dinner would be ready. I told them we had brought dinner with us but nothing to do, Father would be wanting to show his cattle horses etc. to Mr. Kellie and we must stay. Which we did and then on the road home, stopped to visit a little at John Conyers' who had stopped with us sometimes on their road to Hastings and altogether had a very pleasant trip.

The new wheat grew and thrived and many passers by declared it the finest field of wheat they ever saw so we felt quite rich and when Damron came along from Hastings with horses and mules J.T. bought a team of mules from him as we needed more horsepower badly to farm so much land. He hesitated to run in debt for them but Damron felt his money was secure with that fine wheat along the road and urged the matter till finally the deal was made. That was our first big mistake as things turned out and had quite an influence on our future.

The wheat was grand but J.T. had promised to head for Herman Manzer who wanted his done first. Though it was not any too ready J.T. felt he must do so. It was only a couple of days but with a hot wind the wheat ripened fast and the stem was weaker than the other kinds and heads heavy. Then a little hail [came] not enough to hurt anything else. Then Sunday came and J.T. would not cut on Sunday. I urged him to do so as our whole year's work depended on that crop but he would not. Another hot day and heavy wind [and] the wheat was down. They tried but could not get much of it [and] our fine crop did not make 5 bushels to the acre.

The Sunday morning before we headed J.T. went out to the barn to feed. The best mule was lying down. He called sharp to her to get up so he could go between to feed her, [and] she gave a sharp lunge [and] the rope caught her sharply. She fell some way twisted and her neck was broken. Dead in a minute. We had not worked them as we wanted to get more flesh on them for the fall plowing to commence as soon as the wheat was cut. And when we went out the morning the plow[ing] was to begin she [the other mule?] had broken loose found her way to a wheat stack and lay beside it bloated and dead. So in less than a week we were plunged from confidence and hope to poverty and despair.

For everything looked blue to us. We had to have another team or quit farming so much. The windmill and header were not all paid for and we had had to buy a new wagon to haul off our grain the year before, part of it still to pay for and other things, more harness I suppose probably [a] cultivat[or] and another plow as our first one was old and nearly worn out. Anyway we were badly in debt but had not worried as long as our prospects were so good but now it cost more as it took more time to try to save what we could than if the crop had been good.

Expenses seemed to pile up on every hand and we knew not what to do. Naturally J.T. was doing a great deal of figuring these days. Holding the positions he had on the R.R. [he was] intimate friends with contractors and Civil Engineers as well as Bridge Contractors etc. He knew the approximate cost of the Union Pacific, Northern Pacific, B. & M. and other railroads per mile. Knowing they held their charters under plea of public welfare and knowing the cost per mile of freight per mile etc. he was trying to see where R.R. welfare left off and Public welfare began. But he did not bother me very much about it and as I did not attend the Alliance meetings I do not know how early or thoroughly they discussed those topics but they were thinking and every stroke of adversity which robbed us of the fruit of our toil only made them question the more, what if we had had our deserts in other years? And to realize that, had that been so [then] a bad year once in a while could be easily borne. We got through the winter all right owing to the abundance of garden and poultry and having our meat of all kinds. The scarcity of fruit was the only drawback and made us more anxious to raise plenty of fruit ourselves.

Spring came again that of 1883 and except [for] having to renew notes with high interest and compounded at that we did well and got in a large crop in good shape again. And in June Fred was born, prematurely, and for me I came near crossing the divide. Always before I had rallied quickly and got up the third or fourth day but now I did not sit up for 10 days and found myself very weak then. His lower limbs were not well developed and the few women I show him to Mrs. Strohl and Manzer and Aunt Hattie all said he would always be a cripple unable to walk but I felt I could not have it so and without ever thinking of seeing a doctor I used to sit and rub his limbs several times a day and soon had the happiness of seeing them plump out.

This summer Uncle Chester's [family] sold their farm and got ready to move to Wisconsin and as sister Susie had been staying there for some time they arranged to take her with them. How much I desired to have [her] with me no one can ever know but I felt that it would be harder for her [and] that she would have things so much nicer in Wisconsin. And with my 2 babies and all the other work I was afraid I would have to put too much work on her. So I said little about it except to J.T. who would dearly have loved to have her with us had it seemed fair to her to do so. Years afterwards she told me how glad she would have been to have stayed with us but she felt we did not want her. So one never knows and how many mistakes we make sometimes in trying to do right.

They did not go however until after the Old Soldiers reunion which was held in Hastings that fall. They had a tent there and so did O.H. Wrights and Aunt Hattie asked us to come and camp with them. I had never been to one before nor even in a tent and it was hard work to get my 2 babies and the rest of us ready but we managed it and arranged to stay 2 days and one night. I made quite a few new clothes and baked up a lot of food buns roast chickens pies cake etc. besides pickles and jelly.

What a sight it was, the large campground with streets laid out and all the old soldiers registered [so] it was easy to find anyone. They all seemed glad to see us and we had a jolly time. It had been long since we had a night away from home and how strange it was to have no evening chores to do. Instead we went to the campfire where an immense throng of the boys in blue were singing army songs and telling stories of their army life. It was thrilling indeed. Eva Wright and Susie hardly let Jessie out of their arms so I only had Fred to care for the most of the time and he was so good so he was no trouble so I enjoyed every minute until late bedtime for our 3 soldiers. O.H., C.C.

and J.M. kept telling army tales after we were supposed to be asleep.

In the middle of the night it rained a real hard downpour and the tents leaked and tried to blow over and all the men were out in the rain and dark staking them over and I don't know what all. I know with the thunder and all the rain on the tent and people calling it seemed an awful hubbub. And I wished for a house and was dreadfully worried for fear the children's clothes would [get] wet and muddy for water was running in underneath the tent. And the men were trying to bank it up in places and dig ditches and try to keep us dry and we had to roll up the beds and hold the sleepy children etc. etc. But it was kind of fun after all for one night but I never afterward wanted to try a tent for any length of time. Cold in the cool night and unbearable hot in sunshine with flies and dust and mud, there is no minute of comfort.

We all cooked over the same campfire and we all had our teams and fed them corn we had brought and had the cobs to burn and bought some other fuel. It was kind of funny for Aunt Hattie and J.M. would make fun out of anything, but give me a cook stove and a table to put my feet under for more than one meal at a time. I thought often of all the discomforts the soldiers had been through even for 4 long years and it seemed that those who had stayed home and sent them, while enjoying home comforts and becoming wealthy themselves, could never never repay them for their hardships.

As Aunt Hattie would be so busy getting ready to move I undertook to do considerable sewing for her and so pay for a high chair and some other things. The little brown high chair was about as good as new as no one had used it but her Jimmie. It now became Jessie's as it had no shelf and Fred took the red one with shelf I had bought for Jessie and thereafter the youngest took the red chair while the next youngest was promoted to the brown one and to sit by Papa.

J.T. took the job of building a house for Hazelbarth. He had some time before built one for John Ellis and also worked on his barn and on [a] house and barn for Mel Davis. So as we had a lot of farm work to be done we hired a man who had been working on the railroad, Mac Gilbert, to do the plowing etc. He was supposed to be able to do that as well as J.T. and for less than ½ the money but I had many things to do after him or that he neglected. [missing text]

This was the fall the B. & M. built the line west from Kenesaw to Oxford where they joined the valley road to Denver. Before this the terminus had been at Kearney which now from Kenesaw to Kearney became a branch road in effect but was by them declared for some years to be the main line. Whereby they saved a lot of taxes between Kenesaw and Oxford by classing it as a branch line. Over 20 years afterwards when Frank was in High School at Minden someone brought something up in class about Minden being on the main line of the Burlington and Frank corrected them saying it was on a branch line. The professor took it up and ridiculed the idea saying that all the through trains from Chicago to Denver went through there while the Kearney road only had a small train from there to Aurora. He was pretty sarcastic and Frank got rather warm and advised him to get a little information from the County Clerk or Treasurer. He took the advice and apologized very gentlemanly to Frank the next day in class saying that as his mistake had been experted openly he wished to correct it in the same way.

J.T. bought a lot of sheep this fall as Father had done pretty well with them and Willie had to herd them a good deal as well as the cattle and we all had to work very hard. The cattle had been breaking down the corral fences and I had had to run after them a great deal. I was a good runner but they were hard to turn back and I hated to have to leave the babies so J.T. made out to make some new corrals which made life a good deal easier. Nothing is harder than just as you are starting supper and no men home yet to hear the corral fence go smash and have to rush out and run a mile or so back and forth to get them back and then have to fix the fence while the supper burns or gets cold and the children fuss or you fear they will. For children who are used to your running out and leaving them seldom fuss but I always feared they would or [would] get hurt so it was an immense relief to have the corral new again.

Eggs and chickens were much better price than before and I sold quite a lot chickens and some hens to Crandall where we traded at Kenesaw. He shipped them to Denver when the new road opened and got such a good price for them he wanted me to bring as many as I could as they were so fine and he offered me about twice what I had ever had before for them. As we had an old sow a spotted poland china who ate a hen a day I wanted to sell them all off as J.T. would not sell her for she was such a prolific brood sow. They would have brought me a hundred dollars and I proposed to keep it and put it into chickens after we got rid of her and wanted to do so before she got all the young hogs eating them. However J.T. would not allow me to do that and built new pens etc. but to no use. Nearly every day there would be a chicken squawk and I would run out to find another hen being gobbled up. She was so crazy for chickens she would not eat her corn so always had some in the pen and she would stand and make funny noise which the chickens seemed to think was calling them and I am quite sure it was and they would come and get devoured. It was heartbreaking.

J.T. kept working on Hazelbarth's house and Mac Gilbert [did] plowing etc. until one morning just as I had breakfast ready and had called the men and J.T. and Willie were sitting down I realized the water was all gone from the bucket. It was not far to the windmill and when we were alone J.T. usually looked after the water especially if he saw it getting low as he always like myself liked plenty of fresh water at all times especially meal times. But with trying to see if Mac was doing chores right and fixing up things he had not been noticing and I had been bringing the water.

Mac looked into the bucket and seeing it empty took his place at the table without washing. "See here" said J.T. "you have not washed."

"No" was the reply "there is no water."

"Well" said J.T. "no dirty dog shall eat at my table without washing. Go get some water."

"I am not here to carry water" said Mac.

"What? Not to wash yourself with? Has my wife carried water for you to wash your lazy self with? Here get out of here and take your time." And J.T. rose and took out his book where he kept accounts.

"And go without any breakfast?" said Mac.

"Sure I never knew you was such a dirty lazy hound or you never should [have] had a meal here."

"Oh well I will get the water this time" said Mac and went after it.

I had started before but J.T had taken the pail from me and set it down. Mac came in washed and sat down and ate breakfast but before he was through J.T. had risen and got his money and counted his wages out to him. Mac tried to beg off. He did not mind carrying water, he would bring it after this etc. etc. but no use. J.T. marched off and he had to take his wages and go.

Although I liked peace I was glad he was gone for he had been very neglectful of the chores and left many things for Willie and I to do that we had not been told. Mac had dressed better than most hired men and thought himself considerable of a dandy. J.T. had been away early and late so he had not seen so very much of him. I was very glad to see him go and got a young German boy Ernest Shukin in his place.

When they were shingling the house the weather changed and we had a very cold north wind. I worried about the men on the roof and the wind was so icy but still was shocked when J.T. came home to find how very much he was suffering with neuralgia or something in his head and right shoulder and arm. We got on a hot fire and he held his head and shoulder close to it and had it rubbed with liniments and all night we kept hot irons or cloths wrung from hot water around but his suffering was fierce. He had been a sufferer at times from Rheumatism and neuralgia ever since he worked the Northern Pacific R.R. so we thought it would pass off but day after day went by without much relief. J.M. had been over and prescribed all he knew. Some things seemed to give relief for a short time only but day after day and night after night was about the same till finally we sent for old Dr. Gilman and still there was not much change. Of course there was no rest for me at night only while the irons stayed hot.

Then the diphtheria broke out in the county. Mel Davis's [family] a mile from us lost their 3 children. Winklers lost all 5 of theirs. O.H. Wrights lost their only boy Bertie who was almost a young man and finally Uncle Chesters lost their oldest boy George. J.T. was enough better then so we went to the funeral. I am quite sure only J.T. and I went and left the children with Strohls but anyway it was not long till Willie got it and the babies in a lesser degree. As none of the town doctors had had a patient live that we had heard of and Dr. Gilman had we sent for him and he pulled the children through so that by Christmas the doctor considered them out of danger and was not to come again.

We sent for some little gifts for them and the ones for Willie pleased him so much he could not keep still as he should and when we came in the room he was jumping off a chair and rejoicing greatly in being able to play around but though the exercise had only been a few minutes his face turned black and swollen specially his nose and lips and we saw he was on the point of collapse. His heart seemed to stop and luckily we had a lot of hot water. We hurried him right into the boiler of that and with rubbing and some camphor etc. got the blood circulating again. Meanwhile Ernest had started for the doctor who said we had done the right thing [and] that the exercise had started the poison to work and affected the heart and a few minutes' delay would have been fatal.

That was indeed a most terrible winter. We heard of so many deaths around [that] we did not wish to go anywhere and everyone else was about the same. J.T. got cold or something and had a relapse. In fact just as he would seem to get pretty well back he would go again. Ernest was too young really for so much care. There were cows to milk calves to feed and quite a corral full of cattle to care for besides the horses and 3 or 4 hundred sheep and a lot of hogs and the chickens. With so much sickness children and all I could not see after them as usual and the chickens rapidly disappeared.

While I was still in bed the summer before Father's wife Jennie had left him with 3 children. George the age our Jimmie would have been, Mattie the age of our Susie, and Minnie the age of our Jessie. He had considerable trouble getting them boarded here and there so as soon as I got strong enough he brought the girls to stay with me while he kept George with him most of the time. That made me 4 children under 4 years of age to look after and wash for etc. Before the reunion he had hired a family to work for him and taken the girls home and now this winter having gotten a divorce he married a widow woman with 8 children. Meanwhile we had never seemed to get enough for the crops to pay for their production and spite of the fact that we had never bought as much machinery or horses as made things convenient and always made all our household expenses from chickens garden etc. we had so run behind that when we proved up we had had to mortgage the place for $800 at 10% interest. Now as J.T. went from one sick spell to another all winter he felt that he would never be able to do much hard work again and got very despondent.

Of course I tried to cheer him up and never allowed him to think I was discouraged but things sure looked dark. And as the prairie was all sold now around us and being broken up there was really no place there for cattle as our own farm was all broke out and J.T. felt that our cattle and hogs would have to make our living. It did seem that if we would not try to farm at all we would be much better off and indeed if it costs $5.00 an acre to raise wheat and it only brings $4.50 the more acres you have the worse off you are. We at one time envied the Boodys who came out from Iowa with a lot of money lots of fat horses machinery of all kinds and 3 grown young men at home. It seemed they could surely make money but they left after several years of hard work by all [accounts] poorer than they came.

We talked of selling the place and going farther west with the cattle but the many discouraged ones who were always stopping with us on their way east kept us from taking that step.

After his marriage my father stayed mostly at his wife's (Mrs. Manzer's that was) place a mile east and over $\frac{1}{2}$ mile north of us while his timber claim where he had lived since moving back from Kearney was a mile south and $2\frac{1}{2}$ west of us. As he had over a thousand sheep there and other stock he kept going back and forth as although his timber claim had a large sod house on it windmill etc. his wife would not move there but insisted on staying on her place with one room and only a windlass in the well to draw water.

I don't know why she was so stubborn as everything around

there was much better than she had, nice trees and plum and gooseberries and things homelike, while she had nothing but bare prairie.

So one day at dinner J.M. said to J.T. "How will you trade your homestead for my timber claim? Then you would have plenty of room for your stock." I did not suppose J.T. would take it seriously and we women went on talking and visiting about our work as women do but I knew the men were figuring. J.T. would have to plant 10 acres of forest trees to prove up on the timber claim. Though the box elder trees on the north and south were quite large he feared they would not count and they kept on figuring, house here worth so much, the other one so much, well and windmill about [this], every barn so much, [this] here mortgage so much, interest about due on mortgage so much, taxes so much. Well then I heard J.M. say "Well that makes $1300 in your favor. I will assume mortgage interest taxes etc. and pay you so much, $1300 to boot." In all I believe we owed him quite a sum on the sheet and J.T. said "All right I will take it" just like that.

I sure was surprised for he always talked things over with me so much but he felt so sure it was best and I would know it that the deal was made without us women saying a word. Father turned around "Well Lou you will have to get ready to move." It was a late spring and ice and water around. "We will have to get to work as soon as we can." And sure enough the next day we began hauling feed and such things and on March 17 we left our homestead for good and moved back into a sod house again.

Life looked dark only I was glad to be relieved of the mortgage. We both realized that in leaving our first home we had left not only our youth but most of our hope there. While one has youth and hope or either of life, life is not a burden, work is not drudgery but without them it becomes almost unbearable. We realized that the best 7 years of our lives had been given to enrich the B. & M. R.R. That they had cleared annually more from our toil than had been wrung in old times from the colored slaves. The R.R. reports showed a clear profit of over 2 million dollars a month after all expenses just and unjust had been discounted. We know full well that then as now most of the so-called "expenses" were simply money squandered much of it to keep corrupt men in office and to influence legislation. To this end every county had its attorney and physician and even its section bosses were selected more because of their influence than ability. Large salaries were given men who had no ability to do the required work simply because they were somebody's first wife's relation or 32nd cousin to somebody else. And the R.R. "expenses" were enlarged to pay others to do their work. J.T. knew and named many such instances. But even after they had made 4 times the necessary "expenses" had they [only] been content with a profit of 1 million a month instead of 2. If they knowing the farmers were raising their stuff for them below cost of production had said we will divide the profit on each haul of wheat and corn each carload of stock with you we would not only [have] been enabled to keep our place and thousands more like us but would have been enabled to live in comfort and out of debt.

As J.T. often said "We have raised enough grain this year to feed us and all our descendents for a hundred years yet have to sell every bushel of it to pay expenses and our expenses did not include a salary for ourselves or anything not absolutely necessary to produce the crop." These things made us feel bitter and though we were bound to make a good home for the children we felt the lack of youth and hope.

After the bargain was made we felt very sad to think we felt best to leave our first home where we had worked so hard over 7 years and now had it all under plow and apple trees and lilac bushes etc. growing. Where 4 babies had been born and 2 had left us it seemed no other place could ever be so dear. And indeed it was many years before either of us could hardly bear to go by there so in spite of it being the best road to the towns east of us we usually went either north or south of it.

Now we had to move into a sod house again much as I hated and feared them. Every wind that blew always found some dirt to blow off the outside walls and into the house which with little children to creep or play around makes a great deal of extra work. However it seemed to be best so no use to do anything but make the best of it. However we were now real crowded for room so the best was poor enough. J.T. made a trip to Hastings on business connected with selling the sheep I think for our sheep were all-weathers we had bought to winter and fatten. When he came home he told us he had bought 100 5 year old apple trees which would be up on the train to Heartwell the next day. The first house had been built in Heartwell the fall 1883 before by J. W. Hawes who kept a general store there and kept the post office. There was also a general store kept by J. V. Hilman [who] had a hardware and [one by] Howard Brothers, a general store. A hotel [was] run by Mrs. Bingham in a house she had moved from Lowell. In fact several of the houses had been moved from Lowell so that though not 6 months old it was quite a business little place with elevator blacksmith shop etc. and as it was only 5 miles from us we had our mail changed to Heartwell. There was a large business being done as the K.C. & G. R.R. was not built and there was a large territory subject to it on the south.

When they brought home the apple tress there was a whole wagon load of them and they were starting to leave out so the load looked green and they were so large it seemed doubtful if they would live but J.T. was confident they would. We had hired a boy about 16 years of age, Asa King, whose people lived about 3 miles south of us and he dug the holes for them. J.T. trimmed them off at the top some and [made] a new cut on each root. I carried and filled in and Willie hauled water and watered them so we made quick work of it as J.T. had marked where each tree was to set before it got there. We set them in a nice low spot west of the house between some sod walls J.M. had for a hog pasture and every one lived and made a fine growth that year.

J.T. had bought a couple of hundred strawberry plants for me to make up for the bed I had left that I had put so much work on and never had any fruit. He bought the cresent[?] and something to fertilize it and I hurried greatly the afternoon after we got the apple trees set to get the strawberry plants out before it rained as I could see a rain coming up and it would save a good deal of labor in watering to set them then. I got them finished and grabbed a tub and ran quite a distance to where J.M. used to feed sheep to get a tub full of cobs before they got wet and it was raining quite smartly when I reached the house.

And then I saw strawberry plants in the house on the floor and here came little Jessie with her hands full of the plants panting and saying "I hurried Mama so they would not get wet and here they all are." I sure felt like crying I was so tired but one look at the little earnest face so glad she could help settled that and a good laugh at the ridiculous situation followed and another one when J. T. came in. And many many times since when [the] children have done wrong without meaning to I have thought of those strawberry plants. For of all the children I ever knew Jessie was the least mischievous.

One of the first things J. T. busied himself about was getting a school for the children. I do not know sure but think they had to organize District 54 first as we had formerly been in Eaton District with school house over 3 miles away and now Michaels, Terwilligers, Morris[es] and ourselves had children too young to go so far. Morris, Terwilliger and Kellie were the school board with J. T. Director and during the summer they let the contract for the school house and had everything ready by September for school. And to this day there had been very little time without a Kellie on the school board.

Our trees grew finely. Although so large to move we did not lose one then nor for several years. The only thing that reconciled me to giving up our home and living again in a sod house was the trees. Four rows of box elders on the north side of the place 2 rows on the south and a cottonwood grew on the N. E. corner. The box elders were set in 1875 so were large enough to be ornamental and give a nice shady place for the children to play. And they certainly enjoyed playing there with a swing and play house in the shade. Never having lived in a prairie country before my eyes had hungered for the sight of green trees and to have the children be obliged to play in the sun or in the house seemed too pitiful when I remembered the shade and play houses of childhood in the east. J. T. sympathized with me in that although he longed more for the water of the river and lake where he was young.

Still worse was the dearth of fruit. Grandpa Sanford had made us standing offers of barrels of apples whenever we would pay the freight but it was so high it was prohibiting. So year after year went by and the children all over the country probably did not average a half dozen apples a year and no other fruit at all except dried. This seemed a terrible thing to us especially as I remembered the enjoyment at Grandpa Sanford's of going to some kind of berry patch or apple tree at all times almost and the cellar full of every kind of jell jams preserves and bin after bin of apples.

So this was the goal towards which we bent all our energies to make a home in fact which the children would remember with joy. So we set out grapes raspberries and everything we could that we fancied would prolong the fruit season denying ourselves many needed things to pay for the plants and working *overtime* to tend them.

J.T. did not get over his neuralgia very well. Nothing seemed to ease him much except heat. A little overwork or despondent spell meant a wakeful night of suffering and few indeed were the nights until real hot weather and even then sometimes that I did not have to heat irons or bags of salt to relieve his pain in head and shoulder. So we had to keep a hired man a good deal and Willie was constantly with the cattle though we tried to get him a few hours off on Sunday.

We had our own stock and enough others to make a herd of over 100 head so it was a big job for a boy of his age but we did not realize it then.

J.T. would take the wagon occasionally and drive around and buy up calves large enough to wean usually giving them $5.00 for them. This he kept up for many years whenever he had money to spare. He sold his flock of sheep in April or May to a man in from Omaha and we really made some on them but a reporter for a paper got hold of it and made a great thing out of it. Exaggerating the number of sheep and the profit also and finishing by saying that if other farmers had the foresight and etc. of Kellie the country would be in a much better situation. We laughed a good deal about it as really the profit had not been large and the expense for shed corral etc. was considerable besides all the trouble all winter but some thought it true I suppose.

★ STAND UP FOR NEBRASKA ★

THERE ARE those who think the work of the Nebraska Farmers' Alliance is ended; that while the bankers of the state keep up their organization with the avowed purpose of "better influencing legislation" in their behalf, while the merchants, manufacturers, lawyers, doctors, men of every trade or profession, find it to their interest to keep up organizations to aid each other and look after their political welfare, the agriculturalists of the state and nation have no interest in common sufficient for the existence of an organization, but should leave their financial and political business for office seeking politicians to look after. It grieves us to think how little has been accomplished by the Alliance compared with all that is necessary to be done before the farmers of the state obtain anything like justice. At times we grow weary and discouraged when we realize that the work of the Alliance is hardly begun, and that after the weary years of toil of the best men and women of the state we have hardly taken a step on the road to industrial freedom. We know that although we may not arrive there *our children will* enter into the promised land, and we can make their trials fewer and lighter, even if we live not to see the full light of freedom for mankind. We work in the knowledge that our labor of education is not in vain, some one, sometime, will arise and call the Alliance blessed. Meanwhile to us who have learned "to labor and to wait" there come sometimes sweet glimpses of the land beyond, and it seems so near, the road so short, that we can not have long to wait to enter and possess the land.

There's a land where the toiler is free,
　　Where no robber of labor can come,
Where wealth gives not power to oppress,
　　Nor another man's labor to own.

In that sweet by and by
　　Which has been for long ages foretold,
In that sweet by and by
　　Moral worth will rank higher than gold.

We can dwell in that land of the free,
　　If we will, in the near by and by;
We can soon wrest the scepter from gold.
　　We can make labor free if we try.

Vote no interest whatever to gold,
　　Vote for naught which will favor a class,
Make an injury offered to one
　　The most vital concern of the mass.

It does not seem as if that would be hard to do, nor that the road to the promised land of freedom need be long; yet there is a shorter one given by a noted guide hundreds of years ago. But they say, he was visionary, and his way impracticable. It was simply "Do unto others as ye would they should do unto you." The Christian way closely followed at the ballot box would soon right every legalized injustice, and yet the majority of the voters pretend to be his followers. Had they been so in deed and in truth how different would be the condition of our country. We have annually seen the greater part of the wealth produced in the state legislated out of the hands of the rightful owners and into the pockets of those who are allowed to eat, although they *will not* work.

The condition of the farmers of the state has changed greatly in the last three years.

Then the abolishment of high rates of interest on money and reduction of freight rates was all the average Alliance member desired. Thousands of farmers who would have preserved their homes if they could have obtained that relief at that time have now had the mortgage cleared off their farms by the sheriff and are today without a home, and they now demand that *occupancy and use shall be the sole title of land.* So with the transportation question. While a slight reduction would have satisfied three years ago, the people now know that they have the constitutional right to take the railroads, under right of eminent domain and run them at cost in the interest of *all the people*; and never again will any party arouse any enthusiasm among them who advocate less.

Of course the renter does not care greatly for anything which does not free him from the servitude of giving one third or one half his labor for the *chance* to work on the earth. The farmers comprising this organization are the wealthier class of the farmers of the state, and doubtless most of them own land and a home; but if we do unto others as we would they should do unto us we must look out for the interest of our neighbors, who are mostly renters. This is now a state of renters, and the politicians will find they have a new factor to deal with, and that the rapidly increasing number of renters is proportioned very like that of the stay at home vote. And it is reasonable that any man should stay at home unless he sees some hope of benefiting himself by going to the polls. A renter does not care greatly for transportation charges. He who owns the land owns the man who works it, and as soon as freight rates go down the prices rise [and] the renter is raised in proportion. So also he regards the money question. If the value of his products is increased by increasing money volume the rent is raised in proportion so as barely to allow him to exist to produce more. He has no hope of education for his children, or of giving them a better chance in life than he has until he is permitted to go upon the unoccupied land of the state and make for himself a home while adding yearly to the state's productive capacity and wealth. It will soon be necessary for any organization political or social that wishes the renters' allegiance, to advocate occupancy and use as the sole title to land. And if they desire the allegiance of those who, owing to an insufficient money volume, have become debtors, they must advocate a sufficient medium of exchange so that no usury interest will be exacted for its use. The Alliance must not ask if an idea is popular, but rather is it right? If right advocate it, agitate it, write it, speak it, vote it. We can make it popular.

If we wish the farmers to join and keep up this society we must convince them each and every one that it will benefit him individually. We should take a decided step forward in co-operative work. We can compel the building of a co-operative road to the Gulf. We can get an agent to contract the crops of the state at foreign markets for better prices. We can by ordering machinery, flour, coal, etc., in large quantities get greatly reduced prices, and we ought to place ourselves on a level with the Grange and F.M.B.A. in these respects, then each member can soon receive a benefit and a new impetus be given.

Some think the People's party has taken the place of the Alliance. It has to some extent, but cannot entirely.

Leaving out business co-operation which a political organization will not touch, the Alliance has an educational work to perform which no political party can do. Politicians are notoriously cowardly, and not over truthful, especially the law-interpreting class which make speeches for them, and the people will not put faith in them or be taught by them.

A farmer can teach his brother farmers much better the principles of political economy and what he needs to better his condition than the most silvery-tongued office-seeking lawyer that ever lived in any party. There is a large class (yearly becoming larger) who put no faith in political organizations of any class, as regards benefiting the toilers. They think as soon as the party attains power politicians will crowd to the front who care only for the "spoils of office," and the wishes of the voters will be ignored. The Alliance must make it its future work to educate this class to demand the Referendum and direct legislation. It is an excellent time to show the folly of placing one-sixth of the legislative power in the hands of a corrupt governor and president.

If this is to become a government by the people, they must have the right to initiate new laws and not have important questions tabled by a committee appointed by some scoundrel in the shape of a speaker. No power higher than the vote or veto of the people can exist in a free country. The Nebraska farmers and toilers whose productive labor has made the state all it is, whose labor will make it all it ever will become, should stand up for Nebraska by showing what wealth has been produced from her fertile soil and the vast amount paid by her each year to foreigners for the privilege of using the highways of our own state, and as interest money borrowed to replace that legislated from the pockets of our farmers.

Had the farmers of Nebraska obtained justice ten years ago not a dollar of foreign capital would now be drawing interest in the state. That is the sole reason why the loan agents oppose every effort to increase the price of Nebraska's products.

> Stand up for Nebraska! from the hand of her God
> She came forth, bright and pure as her own golden rod.
> Sweet peas and wild roses perfumed all the air.
> Her maker pronounced her both fertile and fair.
> Not a boodler or pauper disgraced the state then;
> Stand up for Nebraska and cleanse her again.
>
> Stand up for Nebraska! and shame upon those
> Who fear the extent of their steals to disclose.
> Who say that she cannot grow wealth or create;
> But must coax foreign capital into the state.
> Such insults each friend of the state deeply grieves:—
> Stand up for Nebraska and banish her thieves.
>
> Stand up for Nebraska, and ope' her jails wide
> To receive all who force us our crops to divide;
> For when we've divided our hard worked for grain,
> Next year we're compelled to divide up again
> With others whose labor no wealth doth create.
> Stand up for Nebraska; drive them from the state.
>
> Stand up for Nebraska, so fertile and fair,
> 'Tis no fault of hers that her granaries are bare;
> For the wealth that her farmers each year do create
> Is more than at present is owned in the state.
> Stop the thieving and quickly her wealth will enhance;
> Stand up for Nebraska and give her a chance.
>
> Stand up for Nebraska. Clear up the disgrace
> Of giving the vile, lowest thieves highest place.
> That our children may honor the good and the true
> We must set an example, and honor them too.
> None but men of high honor in power we must place
> Stand up for Nebraska, clear up her disgrace.

Stand up for Nebraska, and, like Governor W——te[?],
Let her say what shall pay off the debts of the state.
Let the vile baseborn traitors who enslaved her beware;
Their scheme is unfolded, we know why and where
They made our crops worthless, to be England's gain,
Stand up for Nebraska, raise the price of her grain.

Stand up for Nebraska. In the center she lies.
The most valuable jewel 'neath the fairest of skies.
So favored by nature, her vile man-made laws
We find of her poverty are the sole cause.
Let her own her own highways and a road to the south:
Stand up for Nebraska by your votes, not your mouth.

Stand up for Nebraska! Let no foot of her soil
Be held by the idlers to tax rent from toil.
Bid the hard-working tenants of other states come,
And build on each wild quarter section a home.
And soon the world over the watchword will be,
Stand up for Nebraska, the home of the free.

—Mrs. J.T. Kellie

Kellie delivered this speech at the January 1894 meeting of the Nebraska Farmers' Alliance. It was reprinted in this form in the Alliance Independent *on January 11, 1894.*

*Political
Memoir*

Secretary, Historical Society of Nebraska

IN TURNING the records of the old State Alliance into your hands I wish to give a little account of my stewardship.

Although I had been writing for publication in various papers on Alliance and Populist topics for several years I had never felt able to attend a State Alliance Meeting until January [?] 1894. As Hastings was so close and J.T. Kellie (my husband) was a delegate and wanted me to go with him I went as I was very anxious to see those whom I felt I knew by their writings.

Someone had requested me to prepare an article and as the Republicans were just then accusing us of slandering the State and hollering "Stand up for Nebraska" I took that for my subject.

I was greatly interested in all the proceedings and to meet so many hitherto unknown friends and read my article at the evening open meeting and was quite surprised on going to our hotel to find 4 or 5 reporters from Hastings, Lincoln and Omaha papers wanting a copy. As I had not expected anything like that I only had the one copy I had read but they took it and divided it up in portions so all could write at once.

The next day nearly everyone I met congratulated me on my address which seemed to have made a hit.

The next day after report of [the] committee on Jurisprudence [was] made and adopted an address was made by J. E. Thompson representing the State Labor Congress and 10 delegates were appointed to that congress. The Resolutions committee of which J.T. Kellie was one reported and [the] report [was] adopted and committee discharged with thanks of the order. Election of officers followed resulting in election of Senator W. F. Dale of Harlan [County] for President, Prof. W. A. Jones of Adams Vice President. Mr. Kellie was acting doorkeeper and the Kearney County Delegation was on the opposite side of the hall from where I was sitting as an interested spectator only and caring for baby Lois. Nothing had ever entered my thoughts of any personal interest in the election of officers until after the voting for Secretary had well begun [and] some members of the Kearney County delegation (I have forgotten whom) came to me and asked if they could nominate me for Secretary. I replied that I did not know, what did Mr. Kellie think? He had said do as I please they said. Well I thought of course I did not stand any chance and did not like to oppose Miss Buckman but he said Kearney County felt they ought to give me a complimentary vote anyway. So he went back in time to cast Kearney's vote for me and after that several other counties voted the same so there was no election the first ballot but the second was almost unanimous for me.

I was fairly dazed as I did not know whether I was capable of conducting the office or not. I had for some years been secretary of my Alliance 1772 and Kearney County Alliance but neither of them involved much labor and I was sure even then that the State organization would and my hands were very full and if I had extra time when others were asleep I would rather devote it to writing for the papers as I had been doing than to bookkeeping of which I knew very little.

James Cameron of Furnas [County] was elected Treasurer. John H. Powers Lecturer and Executive Committee I. N. Leonard of Lancaster, C. M. LeMar of Saunders, E. E. Soderman of Phelps, L. W. Young of Furnas and J. M. Dimmick of Franklin. Rev. J. M. Snyder of Wherman was elected Chaplain by acclamation. I. N. Thompson of Furnas Doorkeeper, A. E. Farris of Greeley Assistant Doorkeeper and W. O. Dungan of Kearney Steward in the same way. W. F. Wright [was] elected by ballot as delegate to the National F.A. & I.U.

The elected officers were installed by A. Wardell of the National Alliance and the meeting at once adjourned and the new officers and Executive Committee were called at once to meet in executive session. Miss Buckman and A. Wardell met with us and the first thing the President of the Executive Committee said "Well sister Kellie you will have to move to Lincoln." Some others expressed the same idea. But I was frightened. I did not know what the salary would likely be but was sure it was not enough to support our large and growing family in Lincoln.

While on the farm we had lots of fruit vegetables and poultry with stock of all kinds for meat etc. I knew to live in a town where everything was to buy and better clothes [were needed] too we could not do it so I said quite firmly "No I cannot move to Lincoln." Still some of them said it would be necessary as I could not conduct the trips for Lecturers and keep track of things any place else and it would be necessary to have daily mail at least, while we were 5 miles from town.

Everything had been done so quickly I had not had time to talk to Mr. Kellie about anything and was glad when he spoke up and said "They all knew where she lived when they elected her, but if the Executive Committee think she cannot tend to the office where we live she would best not qualify by putting up bonds but let them appoint someone else." Well that did not suit some of them and we adjourned to think and talk over ways and means and find out what was best to do. Incidentally I had found out that Miss Buckman received $8.00 per week and the Alliance had had to rent office and light fuel etc. all in addition. A. Wardell now offered her a better position in the National Office of the Aid Degree at Topeka at $10 per week and she accepted. So I did not have to feel bad about taking her place and we had considerable correspondence for some years.

Well at the next meeting no one was willing to have me resign and we had talked over what we could do as of course we realized that the business if accepted must be done so as not to delay the work of the order. Our house was small being only a wing of the original design and containing three bedrooms on the first floor with a half story over one room and a basement under the 3 bedrooms. One of these bedrooms about 7 x 11 feet had an inside and outside entrance with two windows.

I told them I would clear everything out of it and make it the office and it could be kept locked when not in use. We would not charge anything for rent light or fuel as it was part of our dwelling and J.T. agreed to make two mail sacks from heavy denim like government sacks only smaller and put rings and straps and locks on them and we would keep one key and the Postmistress one and the boys would carry the mail daily to meet morning mail and bring back the incoming mail.

This was done and the 10 mile trip taken daily for several years but no cent ever changed or received for it though no storm ever delayed our daily mail. As we had a fast pony the boys were never long on the road but often the morning mail brought urgent letters from Lecturers or someone so another trip was taken to the post office to get off on the first train out.

Some of the Executive Committee went to Lincoln and packed such things as they saw fit and shipped to Heartwell but left many things as they thought the freight charges would be more than they were worth. Consequently I never received many of the old records which must have been in the office nor any furniture except some open pigeon holes which they called a cabinet and the type writer. Chairs tables etc. were all left.

When I saw the number of large blank books I was indeed dismayed. I was certain I could keep track of money coming in and going out correctly but what to do with all those books I could not imagine especially as the Chairman of the Executive Committee wrote me there were so many blank books "Now you see what you are in for." Naturally I soon found many of them were filled and I packed them away but those that had recent dates in I kept out. Finally I took the record of my Alliance and followed it through the books and then Kearney County and so got an insight of some of what I was supposed to record. But whether I [got it] all right I never knew but no one found any fault. I know I did not use any red ink and suppose I should [have] but did not know what difference it made so did not buy any.

I soon found that the Alliance had been going down much faster than I had supposed as Kearney County was still active. In fact it was the banner county having sent more dues into the State Alliance than any other county. This we attributed to sub-state political action for Alliance work.

I found that prior to January 1889 there were 230 Alliances formed. In December 1890 there were over 2000 Alliances with membership of over 65,000 reported and with 900 delegates.

In January 1892 there were only 647 delegates and in January 1894 when I was elected the number of Alliances (nor members) was not reported but there were only 76 delegates and practically all in good standing were represented.

Within a few days Hon. J. H. Powers came to see us and urged immediate action on printing a lot of manuals for use of the sub Alliances thinking that discussion of those topics was the only way to revive interest and hold the Alliance together. He wished to take the field as Lecturer immediately while the

farmers had some leisure time and said that President Dale favored the action. So I gave an order to Kock & Montgomery of
Hastings for 1000 cloth covered manuals for $35.00 thinking the
President, Lecturer and Secretary would have that much authority and the need was urgent. For this I got called down very
promptly and hard by [the] President of [the] Executive Committee so I told him I would pay it out of my salary. He replied
that they did not like to do that but I must spend no more
money without consent of the Executive Committee which was
pretty well scattered over the state. As it happened there was
never enough come in to pay my salary so I really paid it anyway.
W. F. Wright and H. P. Sayles took the field to reorganize
Alliances and got their pay from the Aid Degree Lodges which
they established in connection but the Secretary had to arrange
for their meetings etc. Hon. J. H. Powers also took the field and
expected the Secretary to keep in daily touch arranging dates
plan[ning] for route and finding friends to entertain and urging
members in the vicinity to turn out etc. He agreed not to ask a
salary but to make out with what the various sub Alliances and
friends donated. His report for a year showed [ ] days [ ] Expenses [ ] Received [ ] less expenses.

It was agreed by all that we must have new constitutions
printed. After considerable correspondence enough advertising
was procured to pay for them.

December 19 and 20 1894 we had the annual meeting at
Kearney. Welcomed by Mayor, responded to by an address by
W. F. Porter, Secretary's report showed $96.75 collected by as-
sessment for D'Allemad.

Received fees and dues	$329.58
National Dues	18.00
Postage	47.60
Money Order	1.05
Printing Expense Office Supplies etc.	

Left $287.80 as Secretary Salary for 50 weeks and balance
due $117.20.
Election of officers resulted.

State Officers
W. F. Dale President
W. F. Porter Vice President
Luna E Kellie Secretary
James Cameron Treasurer
W. F. Wright Lecturer
J. M. Snyder Chaplain
W. O. Dungan Steward

Executive Committee
J. M. Dimmick
F. G. Wilke
T. A. Donahue, Sartoria

Immediately on adjournment of meeting the new Executive Committee issued an appeal to be sent to all state Alliances and other labor organizations by the Secretary soliciting relief for the drouth-stricken sufferers. With appropriate editorials this was printed in over 100 leading agricultural papers and was the first appeal from an organized body from this state. These articles were credited with bringing more aid into the state than any other action but through the decision of the powers in control no aid was allowed to be sent except through the republican organization. Full account will be found in Secretary's report in Nebraska F.A. & I. U. of January 1896.

We had felt the need of direct communication with members so keenly that the Executive Committee at regular meeting May 7 1895 appointed the Chairman and Secretary to see what could be done about starting a state paper and to start one "if it can be done without debt to the Alliance." Also "That authority be given to use ½ the fees and dues for the support of the paper, each member to be a subscriber and have the paper free."

We had in mind a paper such as was run by the Colorado Alliance in Denver by Secretary Southworth and corresponded with him and others about it. Also the Executive Committee authorized or requested the Secretary to write to Senator Allen, Governor Holcomb and other politicians who owed their positions to the Alliance members and solicit aid from them in the paper's behalf. This was done and Senator Allen sent $25, Governor Holcomb $10 and someone else $5. Which ended that.

Finally having secured some advertising the Secretary assured the Executive Committee she would assume all indebtedness for six months' trial or until the annual meeting and the paper was started. J. G. Richmond of Minden did the printing using some of his editorials. I drove one horse down to Minden once a month on press day taking baby Helen five months old at first issue who played in the waste basket or laid on a pile of papers all day while I folded and directed papers. We paid $10 per 1000 papers for 2000 or more each issue till annual meeting. Annual Meeting held at Grand Island December 31 1895. Secretary's report showed

Fees and Dues	$102.64
Order books	1.00
Relief Fund	92.28
Donated Stamps	5.50
Badges	1.20
	$202.62

Expenditures	
Relief	$ 92.28
Treasurer's Expenses	2.50
Bills and Circulars	3.75
Express	.75
Stationery	5.75
Postage	23.01
Printing F. A. & I. U.	
½ Fees and dues from July	19.50
Secretary	55.62
	$202.62

State officers [were] elected.

As it was quite inconvenient to drive to Minden 12 miles on a set day each month come rain or shine we bought an old Washington Hand Press and some secondhand type and moved the paper out to Orchard Farm five miles S.E. of Heartwell. We hired a printer Fred C. Ayers now deputy in one of the State Offices and kept him until we thought we could manage to set and print the paper by ourselves which we would have to do if done at all for funds were very scarce.

Without the advertising especially of the Alliance Aid and Mutual Insurance Companies we could not have gotten out an issue as that was practically all our income. So we went through the winter and till the next September when owing to much orchard work and little interest being shown we suspended the paper. But on getting a contract for advertising and the Executive Committee wishing we started up in the spring under the head of the Prairie Home.

We were not able to pay National Dues and so few Alliances were in good order the name F.A. & I.U. seemed a mockery. However we thought we might work for the Prairie Homes of the state. About this time we got a contract on lowest bid for a large amount of job printing for a Mutual Company which helped greatly.

The Annual meeting of the State Alliance was called to order by President Cravath in Hastings December 31st 1896. Report of Secretary Treasurer showed a total receipt of $143.03 and a total expenditure of $131 with no allowance of salary for Secretary.

Election of officers resulted.

Motion made to change the name of the order to the Farmers' Cooperative Alliance resulting in deciding to submit the question for vote to all Alliances in good standing and the meeting was adjourned till January 12 1897 to await their decision.

At that meeting the sub Alliances being in favor of proposed changes they were adopted.

Quite a large amount of literature was sent out by the office on organizing cooperative companies and many were started from time to time, most of which on account of inexperience etc. did not live many years but a number still live and and flourish and are doing good work today. Most of these in organizing took in members who did not belong to the Alliance so naturally their business meeting took the place of Alliance meetings and no dues were paid to State Alliance.

In May 1897 having arranged for considerable Insurance advertising the paper was started up as the Prairie Home. There does not seem to have been any State Alliance meeting in the winter of '96 and '97 but one was called at Kearney May 24 1898. There was a meeting of National Aid Association at Hastings December 14 1897. This had formerly been the Alliance Aid Degree but owing to stagnation of the Alliances they had changed the name and took in members not belonging to that order. I took a commission as organizer though I could not be away from home more than one night at a time at most as Mr. Kellie was laid up all winter with sciatic rheumatism. I put in two very good lodges, one at Heartwell and one at Keneshaw.

At the meeting at Kearney May 24 1898 very few were present except those living in Buffalo County. Report of Secretary showed

Receipts carried over	$12.03
Fees and dues	43.85
Constitutions	.50
	$56.38

Expenditures	
Prairie Home ½ fees and dues	$22.17
Constitutions (New constitutions necessary on account of change of name etc.)	10.00
Postage	18.00
Stationery	6.00
Circulars	12.00
	$68.17

or $12.89 more than receipts with no salary for Secretary.

S. S. Bears was elected President but no special business done and a meeting called in Omaha June 18 1898. This meeting did not materialize.

The Populist National Committee meeting met [June] 14 and 15 at which I was present and the National Reform Press of which I was a member met June 13 and 14th. Accounts of both appeared in Prairie Home.

Another State Alliance meeting was called for Kearney first part of July 1899. Being sick in bed [I] was unable to attend. I sent books and reports either to George Biechel or S. Bears I think but no report was ever made to me as to what was done and the books were not returned. I never asked for them and do not know that a meeting was held. Think not, at least I was not told of any new election of officers.

In 1900 Mr. Kellie and I were delegates to the Cincinnati Middle of the Road Populist convention and again met with National Reform Press Association which is one of the pleasant memories of life.

Coming home we worked with all our might for Barker and Donnelly and [I] received nomination [as] Populist Candidate of Public Instruction on the state Ticket nominated at Grand Island. This was an unexpected honor but accepted on urgent request of the Labor Unions of Omaha as they said they could get a larger vote for someone so well known.

Then when Asa Taylor, the head and in fact nearly all of the Union Reform movement, died from overwork the next spring both daughter Jessie and myself felt our last chance was gone. Hardly a reform paper remained alive and the abuse was hard to bear. Jessie now 19 had given the largest part of 5 years to the paper work with hardly a cent of pay and no time for pleasure. Midnight found her working 3 or 4 times a week and sometimes all night but now we both felt that all our work was useless.

In order to keep the paper alive we had changed to a local and [being] full of local news got us many subscribers in both parties. Also local advertising was coming in enough so that we knew that we could at last make a living from the paper. But that did not appeal to us. We had hoped to bring better conditions for the coming generation and now knew that disorganized and discouraged as the old workers were there would have to be another generation grown to take up the work.

So Jessie gave up and I hired a local editor and we went back to the farm. I was supposed to send in editorials but to save my life I could not say anything that I felt I had not said before and had not done any good. So in a few weeks heartsick and discouraged I asked the local editor what he would give for the outfit and when he offered about ½ what it was worth but said he did not have much money but would give secured notes. I gladly took him up and have never written a word for publication to this day. In fact I found myself a physical wreck and it was over 10 years before I had regained my health. And I dared not even think of what hopes we had had. It meant sleepless nights and nerves completely unstrung.

Mr. Kellie who had always urged me to work for the cause saw my condition more fully than I did and seldom allowed the subject to be mentioned. On the contrary he arranged to begin the much-needed addition to the house which helped occupy my time.

And so I never vote [and] did not for years hardly look at a political paper. I feel that nothing is likely to be done to benefit the farming class in my lifetime. So I busy myself with my garden and chickens and have given up all hope of making the world any better.

Luna E. Kellie

★ AFTERWORD ★

WOMEN HAVE been writing their own histories for a long time. They have written them for their children and for their friends. Because women's histories have often been overlooked, a wealth of information has been left untapped. Although Luna Kellie has been mentioned by historians interested in Populism, their focus has been on the political movement, not on Kellie's own description of how she became motivated to join the Farmers' Alliance and to participate in the Populist party.

Luna Kellie's 160-page personal memoir, written about 1925 when she was 68 years old, and her political memoir about her involvement with the Farmers' Alliance together provide a fairly complete account of her political activities and home life from the time she was eighteen until she was forty. Her writing reveals her living conditions, familial networks, the division of labor in her home, and women's roles in the Farmers' Alliance and the Populist party. Her accounts help explain what motivated women to become involved in politics. Furthermore, they illustrate how the Middle-of-the-Road Alliance movement—so-called because members took a middle ground between the Republican and Democratic parties—evolved, prospered, and then died when "fusion" proponents pushed for major-party alignment.

Women actively participated in the Farmers' Alliance and the Populist party, officially the People's party. Yet little of the scholarship on the Farmers' Alliance and the Populist movement does justice to the active and complex role women played.

Historians have tended to focus on male political figures or on a few flamboyant female characters, such as Mary Elizabeth Lease, who is known for urging farmers to "raise less corn, and more Hell."

Luna Kellie's accounts about her life on the Nebraska plains and her later political activity are perhaps one of the most complete accounts of the Mid-Road political faction available to readers. It is unfortunate that political historians have not ventured to examine her memoirs more closely.

Five major turning points in Luna Kellie's life trace a circle of hope and despair: (1) she is filled with hope about the prospect of a home, family, and financial stability and leaves for the Nebraska plains with her husband from an urban, crowded St. Louis; (2) the Kellies meet with intense personal and economic hardship, losing two children as well as their homestead; (3) the Kellies realize that their economic hardship is caused not by their own failure but by corporate monopolies beyond their control, and they join the Farmers' Alliance; (4) Luna Kellie becomes secretary of the Farmers' Alliance and prints the *Prairie Home* newspaper for several years; (5) Luna Kellie becomes extremely disillusioned with Populism, the Farmers' Alliance, and politics altogether.

Kellie's Early Life

Luna Elizabeth Sanford, the eldest of five children, was born June 9, 1857, in Pipestone in the southwestern corner of Minnesota, where she spent her childhood. About 1869 her family moved to Lansing, Minnesota, where Kellie's father, James Manley Sanford (known as J.M.), worked building the Northern Pacific railroad line. Luna's family lived in a rented house in Lansing, and it was there that Luna's mother, Martha Sanford (formerly Martha Lois Smith), first read about the great plains of Nebraska.

The pamphlets distributed by the railroads painted a rosy picture of the Nebraska life. The Chicago Burlington and Missouri pamphlets claimed the company's purpose in distributing information was "to under-state rather than exaggerate the facts

TREMENDOUS CROPS !!!
A SUCCESSFUL REGION !!!

GLAD TIDINGS
FOR THE
FALL AND WINTER OF 1877 AND 1878.

SOUTHERN IOWA
&
SOUTH-EASTERN NEBRASKA,

AHEAD.

THE OLD B. & M. R. R.

HAS THE LARGEST & FINEST CROPS,

THE MOST SUCCESSFUL SETTLERS
THE BEST & CHEAPEST LANDS,
THE LONGEST
CREDITS & LOWEST INTEREST

CHEAPEST FARES & FREIGHTS.

SEE INSIDE.

PLINY MOORE, Agent,
317 BROADWAY,
NEW YORK, CITY.

This B. & M. pamphlet promised settlers in Nebraska the best land, lowest prices, and easiest ground to break. Courtesy State Historical Society of Iowa.

in regard to the B. & M. lands." An 1877 pamphlet said that the crops "are simply immense," that people who settled in Nebraska without capital could become rich if they "fought hard enough." The climate, it said, was "exhilarating, temperate and healthful," while the soil "contained untold wealth." Luna's parents discussed moving to Nebraska, but J.M. Sanford feared his wife would not survive the journey well, and he decided to farm on the outskirts of Lansing.

The family farmed between 1871 and 1872 but they lost money. During the winter of 1872–73 they moved to Austin, Minnesota, where Luna's father worked for a short time before leaving for St. Louis, Missouri, and a job on the Northern Pacific railroad bridge. James Sanford sent for his family in March 1873. In the summer of that year an epidemic of malarial typhoid swept the St. Louis area, and when fall came Martha Sanford died. At the age of sixteen, Luna Sanford was left to tend the rest of the Sanford family.[1]

While Luna was living in St. Louis, she met her father's foreman, a young man named James Thompson Kellie (known as J.T.) who had immigrated from Toronto, Canada. Luna Sanford and J.T. Kellie courted and married December 31, 1874.

J.M. Sanford then took his younger children to Middleton, Wisconsin, and boarded them there so that he could travel to Nebraska to file a homestead and timber claim. After returning, he married a twenty-two-year-old woman named Jennie and moved out to homestead in Nebraska in the spring of 1875.

J.T. and Luna Kellie stayed in St. Louis and had a child, William. At the urging of J.M. Sanford, however, they decided to give up living in town and to buy some farmland near his. Both J.T. and Luna wanted a large family and a house of their own, and the idea of homesteading attracted them.

While J.T. stayed behind to fulfill his obligation to the bridge construction company in St. Louis, the eighteen-year-old Luna set off with her baby on a train to Grand Island, Nebraska, to meet her father and to buy a land ticket. This is the starting point of Luna Kellie's personal memoir. On its pages she comes alive for us, as we relive with her both the mundane and the moving experiences of her family's life on the Nebraska plains.

The Political, Economic, and Social Climate
of the 1870s

The economic and social climate the Kellies were to face in Nebraska was by no means friendly. The seventies in Nebraska are typically characterized as a period in which the state experienced growth beyond what it could accommodate, given the national financial situation. By 1870 Nebraska's population had increased to 122,993 and it was estimated at 250,000 in 1874. However, the seventies were also marked by a severe depression and a drop in crop prices. Economic instability caused by problems in federal coinage of money and by the bankruptcy of major investment firms sent an economic panic through Nebraska in 1873.[2] The prices of grain and livestock plummeted and the assessed value of farmland declined from $4.79 per acre in 1870 to $2.86 per acre in 1879.[3] There were also many natural catastrophes in the 1870s. Swarms of Rocky Mountain locusts descended on fields and ate every living plant in sight, and the state was struck by a drought that only perpetuated the locust problem. Indeed, the locust blight was so severe that the state legislature passed a law requiring "every able-bodied male resident between the ages of sixteen and sixty years, to perform from two to ten days labor . . . in the destruction of grasshoppers."[4] The locusts compounded the drought, and many families moved back east.

This era was particularly frustrating for farm families who worked in parched fields filled with grasshopper eggs. They knew they would be unable to pay their mortgages. Farmers slowly became aware that politicians worked on behalf of the corporations to which they were constantly in debt: the railroads, the banks, and the brokers to whom they were often forced to sell their crops. The Nebraska legislature had imposed no regulations on railroad freight prices or bank interest rates, nor had it expressed any interest in squelching corporate monopolies. It is no wonder that the farmers began to seek political tools to counter these problems. In *History of Nebraska*, historian James Olson explains why:

> The farmer seemed to be disadvantaged wherever he turned. High freight rates reduced the price of his products and in-

creased the cost of farm machinery and other commodities he had to buy. Short of cash, he had to support his purchases with mortgages on his crops or his land. At best, he had to sell his crops immediately after harvest at any price the local speculators were willing to pay. Should his crops fail, he was likely to find himself confronted with a judgment against his land which stood in a fair way to absorb his entire equity. Even in good years he was lucky if he could meet his bills and his debts and still retain title to his land.[5]

Farmers organized themselves to relieve their dire economic conditions first in the Grange, a social and educational reform movement that was formed in 1867 and came to Nebraska in 1872. The Grange grew quickly, and soon members made attempts to organize buying cooperatives. Ultimately, the Grange movement failed because of mismanagement and because economic conditions improved slightly in the late 1870s and early 1880s.

The disappearance of locusts, the relief from drought, and a stimulated business sector eased the severe stress farm families experienced in the middle seventies. In 1875 a new state constitution affirmed the right of the legislature to regulate railroads and restricted the government's right to provide financial aid to corporations. These changes gave farmers some hope that conditions would improve. They were to learn that authorization to regulate railroads did not mean that the legislature would act on the mandate.

Kellie's Life on the Nebraska Plains

The living conditions on the plains were the first of many hardships Luna Kellie encountered. Like many people settling in Nebraska, she had never seen a sod house, the kind of dwelling in which most rural Nebraskans lived. Whereas wealthy farmers and city dwellers had frame houses constructed of wood, most of the new settlers had sod houses. Sod houses were the product of the Nebraska plains environment, which lacked two basic necessities: wood and water. Water could be obtained by drilling a well. But since there was no wood around and lumber was very expensive due to railroad shipping rates, sod houses were the most economically feasible and most efficient forms of shelter. James Olson provides an apt description:

> The walls were made of sod—or "Nebraska marble" as early settlers liked to call it—and the sod house became the enduring symbol of the new frontier. Sod houses varied from dugouts that were little more than caves to rather pretentious, two-story affairs, although the average sod house was a simple one-room, frame-supported structure. The most prosperous pioneers shingled their roofs or covered them with tar paper, but most sod houses were roofed with earth or sod. The hard-packed earth usually served as the floor. Occasionally the inside walls were white-washed or covered with old newspapers, and a cloth was stretched across the top to provide a ceiling. Although far from an ideal place in which to live—the problem of keeping it clean was particularly burdensome—the sod house was fairly cool in summer and warm in winter. Indeed, in these respects it frequently was more satisfactory than the poorly insulated frame house which replaced it as soon as the settler could afford to make the transition.[6]

Initially, Kellie was overwhelmed by the difficulties of living on the plains, from the sod houses that "sickened" her— "dirty looking things"—to the armies of grasshoppers that left "no sign of leaf or stem." She learned, however, to see the beauty in the land, the people, and the life. Her writing abounds with details, from descriptions of the prairie covered with buffalo peas—"really the most lovely sight I had ever seen"—to tales of memorable incidents, like running frantically with her baby from a "bellering" bull. Her accounts of her neighbors are especially telling. In a section Kellie labeled "Callers," we meet the lying mother and daughter who "borrowed" Kellie's quilting pieces as well as the tobacco-chewing Mrs. Strohl, without whose friendship, Kellie says, "I know I must have fainted and dropped by the wayside ere many years had flown."

Though her writing is sometimes sketchy or confusing, Kellie was a natural storyteller. Her accounts of how she and

J.T. coped with disasters, inexperience, grueling physical labor, poverty, and wrenching personal loss need no elaboration. An exploration of the larger context in which they struggled, however, enriches their personal story and helps explain their involvement in politics.

The Political, Economic, and Social Climate of the 1880s

The Kellies were not unique in their inability to make a profit despite very hard work. The 1880s marked a period of increased production; farmers enjoyed excessive rainfall and the amount of food they produced tripled. Despite farm families' optimism that the prosperity would spread to them, crop prices spiraled downward.[7] Simultaneously, industry boomed, and development proceeded at a record-breaking rate in Omaha and Lincoln. The government continued to be dominated by Republicans who, it was generally conceded, pandered to the largest railroads in Nebraska: the Union Pacific and the Chicago Burlington and Missouri.

The 1880s saw more organized discontent. A large body of farmers believed the cause of their poverty lay with railroad monopolies, and they did not need to look far to find evidence. Each town usually had only one railroad line, and its monopolistic characteristics were blatant. In areas served by two or more railroads, business was divided into sections and rates were maintained by mutual agreement. Railroads also successfully resisted the efforts of local governments to tax the land they had been given by the federal government. In addition, railroads fought openly and successfully against legislative efforts to implement the provision in the Nebraska constitution of 1875 that provided the legislature with the tools to regulate the railroads.[8]

Perhaps the most blatant affront to farm families was the railroad's distribution of free passes to every public official who wanted them, a practice commonly known as the free pass bribery system. Although the railroads represented what was most offensive to the farmers' prosperity, the local grain elevator operators also received blame. The operators downgraded the farmers' grain and actively sought to sabotage cooperative efforts by farmers to remove the brokers. Finally, bankers and their mortgages were obviously oppressive to farmers. However, many saw the banking problems as a symptom of the inadequate currency in the United States since the Civil War.[9]

The Farmers' Alliance Comes to Nebraska

Like many other farm wives, Luna Kellie was affected dramatically by these unfair economic practices, and she slowly began to see that politics touched her life very directly. She had been taught, she says, that "it was unwomanly to concern oneself with politics and that only the worst class of woman would ever vote if they had a chance etc. etc." But as her family members sickened and died during their early years on the plains, as crop prices plummeted, and as the family experienced natural disasters, high railroad freight rates, mortgages on their homestead, and near starvation, Kellie looked for the reason behind their difficulties. She and J.T. began to feel that the system was at fault for their financial hardship. This was a cathartic realization because many people in the nineteenth century believed in Social Darwinism, that survival of the fittest determined the success or failure of the individual.[10]

In the winter of 1881, a Farmers' Alliance chapter was organized by W. A. McKeighan in the Kearney area, and J.T. Kellie became very involved. The organization had its roots in the South, where poverty-stricken farmers sought to organize against the crop-lien system of farming. This system gave landlords control over what was farmed and how it was distributed, and farmers were constantly in debt to landowners. The Farmers' Alliance formed farming cooperatives in an attempt to control the selling and purchasing of their own goods. The Alliance fought against corporate monopolies and corporate or foreign ownership of land and supported the free coinage of silver as a means of preventing deflation.

During 1882 the Kellies had many discussions at home about the Farmers' Alliance and political issues. But before

Luna Kellie became actively involved in Alliance issues, her political interest was piqued by the issue of women's suffrage. Her neighbor the Widow Manzer had to ask Luna to ask J.T. to support more schooling, and, Kellie wrote, "Well that started me thinking. . . . Right then I saw for the first time that a woman might be interested in politics and want nay need a vote." At that point, Luna Kellie realized that politics could directly change both her life and other women's lives. And the Alliance, she knew, allowed women to vote as equal members in its organization.

Though Kellie was naive about politics and not well informed on all Alliance issues, the suffrage issue did get her involved in discussions with J.T. and later with others. And though by 1892 she had rejected women's suffrage as an Alliance issue, initially both Kellies thought the Alliance would have to "clean up the polls and make it fit for any good woman to go to." In her memoirs, Kellie rarely refers directly to other Alliance issues, although she mentions suffrage and railroad freight taxes in her brief references to the Farmers' Alliance. She says, though, that the suffrage issue "was only a sample of many of our good natured talks."

Financial Maneuvering

By 1883 political talk in the Kellie family was escalating. Despite their best efforts, they had their most devastating year financially. Counting on a bumper crop of wheat, J.T. had taken out loans for a plow, a header, and a windmill. Unfortunately, the crop failed due to heavy wind just before harvest, and the Kellies plummeted from tenuous prosperity to near bankruptcy. Despite the fact that they managed to pay for household expenses with eggs, chickens, and garden produce, they still had to mortgage their homestead in 1883 for $800 at ten percent interest. They began to think there was no point in doing any farming at all because "if it costs $5.00 an acre to raise wheat and it only brings $4.50 the more acres you have the worse off you are." They considered going further west, but the stream of would-be settlers returning east discouraged them from pursuing that option.

The Kellies were not alone in experiencing what it felt like to have a mortgage to pay. Local Nebraska commentator Barnes Cass describes how the farmer got into debt:

> An actual loan . . . typical of thousands made during those trying periods was a loan of $100 for three months' time. Six percent a month for three months on $100 would amount to $18. This was deducted in advance and the borrower was given $82, and the $18 were divided between the loan agent and the owner of the money, and the deal was satisfactory to all parties. . . . The note signed by the borrower and his wife did not bear interest for three months but after maturity it bore both interest and penalty. To the inexperienced borrower, it looked fair to charge no interest and the accommodation of the money was well worth paying $18 for. The security was on a pair of horses, harness, lumber wagon and corn cultivator. The sequel was the old, old story. The borrower was unable to pay the $100 note at the end of the three months. He was however able to raise another three months' interest or "penalty" to let the note run on. Then followed extensions, not renewals, and partial payment of penalty till finally the end and collapse came. The chattel security was surrendered and sold to satisfy the $100 note.[11]

The Kellies were desperate to get out from under their mortgage. Eventually, J.M. Sanford offered to trade the Kellies' homestead with its mortgage for the timber claim that J.M. owned. Without consulting Luna, J.T. agreed to the deal, and Luna later wrote that she "sure was surprised for he always talked things over with me so much but he felt so sure it was best and I would know it that the deal was made without us women saying a word." Her comment makes it clear that the one-sided decision belied the usual working relationship she had with her husband.

Division of Labor

The division of labor between the Kellies is apparent from the way they perceived their roles in family production. J.T. ac-

knowledged in many overt ways that Luna's work was crucial to
farm production. For example, he gave her two cows and some
pigs as payment for her contribution to the family finances. But
J.T. did not want to "owe" Luna money, and he considered providing for the family in every way his responsibility.

Kellie's earnings from the sale of her eggs and chickens
were significant. In 1880, for example, she brought in $236, a
considerable amount at a time when wages for an able-bodied
farmhand at harvest were $2 a day.[12] She did not expect, how-
ever, to be treated as an equal partner. When J.T. refused to sell
his brood sow and when he traded away their first homestead,
Luna disagreed with his decisions but did not argue. As the division of labor played itself out, Luna deferred to J.T. on major
decisions related to the household economy while J.T. supported Luna's later political activity by providing the labor she
once gave to the household economy.

It is of some interest to compare Luna Kellie's role in her
marriage with the role of women in the Farmers' Alliance. The
Alliance knew that without the political activity of women, they
would nearly cease to exist as an organization. Both the Farmers' Alliance and the Populist party needed women's political
support, and yet often their labor went unpaid and unacknowl-
edged. Although the Alliance supported a woman's right to vote
within their own party, they did not make women's suffrage an
issue in the 1892 convention, leaving Alliance women to fight
for agrarian issues but not for suffrage, which alone would give
them an active voice in political life.

To the extent that J.T. Kellie and the Farmers' Alliance did
recognize the importance of women to family finances and political activity, they were by no means typical for the turn of the
century. As Mari Sandoz points out in *Sandhill Sundays and
Other Recollections*, an account of life on the Nebraska plains, a
woman was often treated no better than a horse, and sometimes
worse. Sandoz writes of women who were enticed to travel
west by marriage ads only to be put to work as personal ser-
vants. In fact, there were men who hobbled "their" women by
tying their legs to prevent their running away, unhobbling them
only when they were pregnant with their first child and could
no longer run.[13]

Even in these relationships, though, it was clear that women were essential to the farm: a man needed a woman to reproduce, cook, clean, wash, garden, and help plow. But women's labor was subsumed by men, and women were never paid. Given this backdrop, one can see the significance of both the division of labor on the Kellie farm and within the Alliance: J.T. acknowledged Luna's cash contribution to their family, and Alliance men allowed women to participate in their organization. However, *allowed* is the operative word. When women held up the institutions that supported men, they were in their proper role. When women tried to escape the role of sustaining men's institutions, they were limited in their participation both in a progressive home and in a progressive political organization.

The Mid-Roaders in Nebraska: No "Movement Culture"?

The Kellies' loss of their homestead and move to Adams County in March 1884 marked the beginning of Luna Kellie's serious support of the Farmers' Alliance. She began to make a conscious connection between her family's financial problems and the railroad companies' general exploitation of farmers (the companies were notorious for charging high shipping rates and influencing legislation regarding railroad freight rates). For the next five years, while devoting herself to making their new timber claim a home, Kellie also educated herself on Alliance issues. By 1889 she was a well-informed participant in the Alliance movement. When the Alliance decided to back the official Populist party, she was ready to play a fundamental role in keeping an anti-fusion branch of the party alive in the 1890s.

The Populist movement in Nebraska was composed of members who supported fusion with the Democrats and those who adamantly opposed it. Luna Kellie's ideas about the Farmers' Alliance and the Populist party represent the middle-of-the-road anti-fusion philosophy of Populism. The term *Middle-of-the-Roader* was coined during the 1892 election campaign to refer to those who felt the best stance for the newly formed Populist party was to reject both the Democratic and the Republican philosophy and to retain what they saw as the integrity of the Populist movement. But as Populism became more partisan in nature with more self-interested politicians running for office, the Mid-Roaders were forgotten by their party leaders.

In *Democratic Promise: The Populist Moment in America*, Lawrence Goodwyn describes the downward spiral of the Populist movement in Nebraska between 1890 and 1900. He suggests that the movement was plagued by so many problems that Populism "in the deepest meaning of mass citizen politics— in the Populistic sense of public life as a shared *experience* of people . . . had no 'movement.' " In essence, Goodwyn believes that Populism could not "be said to have existed there at all." He cites in particular the failure of Nebraska's Populist leaders to organize a stable infrastructure for the movement. He says that Populists in Nebraska suffered from indecisive and factionalized leadership, lack of organization, and a shallowness in what he sees as the base of the Populist strength—"movement culture." Finally, he argues that the majority of Nebraska Populists did not seek remedies for their hardships by forming farmers' cooperatives and educating themselves but relied instead on weak and factionalized leaders.[14]

Goodwyn persuasively argues in *Democratic Promise* that "real" Populism never existed in Nebraska. It is generally true that a statewide cooperative infrastructure which could organize farmers was lacking and that the politicians who emerged as leaders in Nebraska were essentially Populist fusionists or left-leaning Democrats such as William Jennings Bryan. However, Goodwyn's argument overlooks the intensely devoted group of Alliance members and Middle-of-the-Road Populists who actively sought to organize Nebraska farmers into cooperatives and to educate rural people about transportation reform, land reform, and money reform. It is to this latter group that Luna Kellie belonged. The only mention Goodwyn makes of any cooperative movement in Nebraska is in a footnote where he comments: "The only regions of Nebraska producing a political movement genuinely resembling Populism were the handful of counties—none too far from Custer County—which had generated at least the beginnings of a cooperative movement. From such counties came authentic greenbackers, such as Mrs. Luna Kellie, a tireless reform editor, and—a sure sign of the culture of Populism—movement songs."[15]

Mid-Road Populism at Its Height

The intensity and fervor of the Farmers' Alliance political campaign in 1890 are unparalleled in any other campaign in Nebraska history. Addison Sheldon, author of *Nebraska: The Land and the People,* writes, "there has never been such a political campaign in Nebraska as the campaign of 1890, and there never can be such another."[16] A combination of drought, corrupt government, and railroad monopolies inspired farmers to wage a war on Republican and Democratic incumbents alike.

In 1890 farmers experienced one of the worst droughts in Nebraska history. By July 1890 the temperature had registered over 100 degrees Fahrenheit for twenty days out of thirty, and it had risen to 115 degrees on many occasions. The rainfall had diminished from a normal average of twenty-six inches to seventeen and even twelve inches in some areas. Consequently, the crops failed from the western border of Nebraska eastward. By August appeals for food were coming from western farmers in Nebraska who were completely destitute. Farm families put the energy that might have gone into cultivating the land into "raising less corn and more hell" in the campaign of 1890. Sheldon writes:

> The long-endured economic grievances of the farmer class,
> the earnest debates of the Farmers' Alliance in the country
> schoolhouses, the accumulated sense that favored classes in
> Nebraska and elsewhere were living in extravagance upon the
> products of labor carried the cheering multitudes from one
> Alliance picnic to another throughout the length of the
> state. . . . eager crowds by thousands stood from two to four
> hours listening to the fiery orators who declaimed the
> wrongs they suffered. . . . they sang "Good-bye Old Party,
> Good-Bye," "The Mortgage Has Taken the Farm, Mary,"
> and a score of other soul stirring songs. . . . Mrs. J. T. Kellie,
> was the author of many of these songs . . . and became a
> woman leader of prominence.[17]

Luna Kellie naturally fell into the role of contributor to the language of Populism as it developed through the reform press, Alliance songs, and Alliance orators. By 1889 she was corresponding with Alliance members, and by 1890 she had emerged as a songwriter and activist for the campaign of 1890.

The Alliance efforts in campaigning were successful, and the Farmers' Alliance candidates swept the Nebraska House and Senate. They narrowly missed electing John H. Powers as the first Populist governor. Many of the key players in later Alliance politics were elected, including Mid-Roaders John H. Powers and the soon-to-become-famous William Jennings Bryan.

Fusion or Middle-of-the-Road?

Even though the Populists swept the legislature in the election of 1890, they were unable to change the Republican gubernatorial defense of railroad monopolies. The Populists did manage to pass the Newberry Bill (proposed by Representative Fred Newberry of Hamilton County), which called for reducing rates on goods carried on Nebraska railroads to correspond with rates enforced in Iowa. The bill was passed—only to be vetoed by Republican governor James E. Boyd.

The problems that the Populist legislature encountered trying to enact reform legislation were very demoralizing to many Populists. While the legislative setbacks only confirmed Populist Mid-Roaders' belief that they could not trust Democrats or Republicans to effect any kind of change, the other Populists were frustrated by the legislature's inability to obtain more fair railroad shipping rates. The frustration many Populists felt was manifested in the election of 1892. Despite the high level of Populist party activity at the Omaha national convention for the People's party in which the Omaha Platform was drafted, the 1892 campaign did not have the same kind of grass-roots support it had had in 1890 when almost every able-bodied farmer was on the stump for Populism and the Farmers' Alliance.[18] Republican Lorenzo Crounse won the governorship and the Republicans took control of both the Senate and the House in the Nebraska legislature.

After 1892 politics in Nebraska focused on fusion between Populists and Democrats. The Democrats needed fusion in Nebraska to obtain enough votes to get into office, and many fusionist Populists felt that the Democrats could implement some of the changes they desired. The most flamboyant proponent of fusion was the Democrat William Jennings Bryan. Bryan was charismatic and on the very left of Democratic politics. He favored reduced railroad fees and proposed the free coinage of silver to solve the country's financial problems. Bryan was a savvy politician and saw very clearly that he could win the governorship if he could only get the Nebraska Populist vote. He made every attempt to convince the Populists to fuse with Democrats.[19] For that reason, fusion became a hotly debated issue among Populist Alliance members in Nebraska.

There was a split among Populists in Nebraska about the political method by which to achieve their goals. There were those in Nebraska and elsewhere who felt temporary fusion was not a bad strategic move if another party was supporting an issue in which they believed. These fusion Populists insisted they were as sincere in their ultimate purpose as Mid-Road Populists, and they were convinced that temporary fusion was one way of obtaining the political tools with which to change the system. However, Mid-Roaders like Kellie adamantly disagreed with this philosophy because they feared the movement would be co-opted by corporate politicians and would ultimately lose its purpose.[20]

Women's Suffrage in Alliance Politics

Kellie, a strong Mid-Road Populist, began to contribute to Alliance newspapers in the late 1880s. In the April 1892 issue of the *Farmer's Wife*, which was edited, written, and published by Alliance women in Topeka, Kansas, Kellie articulated her ideas about women's suffrage. Her position had drastically changed since her initial involvement with the Populists. Although she had been politicized by concerns about women's suffrage, she supported the party's politically expedient choice not to promote the issue. This change of heart is apparent in her newspaper contributions in 1892.

In the April issue, Kellie was responding to another Alliance woman, Emma Ghent Curtis, who advocated women's suffrage in a National Alliance plank. Curtis had written a poem titled "To a Colored Brother at the Conference," noting the hypocrisy of a black man's opposition to women's suffrage because women had played such a major role in the abolition of slavery. Kellie responded to Curtis's poem with a poem of her own written from the perspective of a black man. Kellie's protagonist in the poem agrees that women's suffrage is a basic human right but argues that a suffrage plank in the National Alliance platform would divide the Alliance too much. The black male in her poem contends that without unity, suffrage would be of no consequence:

> For I stood there a living example
> Of wrongs years of votes failed to right,
> And long years to come yet will fail to,
> Unless all the toilers unite. [21]

Through this man's eyes, Kellie describes how daughters and wives of black men agree that suffrage should take second place to issues members could agree upon. This debate in the form of poems occurred after the National Alliance convention in February 1892, in which the women's suffrage issue was buried in an attempt to bridge the gap between northern and southern elements in the Alliance. [22]

"Stand up for Nebraska"

In addition to her active participation in Alliance dialogue, Kellie served as secretary of both the local Kearney, Nebraska, Alliance and the Kearney County Alliance. She was also destined to play a much larger role in keeping the Farmers' Alliance together in the years between 1894 and 1900.

Alliance members who knew Kellie's writing had asked her to prepare a speech to read at the 1894 state meeting. Her stirring "Stand up for Nebraska" touched upon many of the most sensitive issues the Nebraska Alliance had faced in the past years. Foremost was the concern that fusionist Democrat William Jennings Bryan would steal Populism away from Populists.

William Jennings Bryan represented the First District in Congress in 1891 and again in 1893, when he lobbied conservative Democrats to support free coinage of silver. In 1894 he obtained a powerful position as editor of the Democratic paper the *Omaha World-Herald* and waited for his chance to swing the Democratic party to the left. Bryan had gained some fusionist Populist support and announced his candidacy for the U.S. Senate. In a politically savvy move, he also supported fusionist Populist Silas A. Holcomb in his bid to become governor. Holcomb won the governorship, and although Bryan did not win the Senate seat, he did win control of the Democratic party, imposing the free-silver issue upon old-school Democrats and forcing them to support fusion. Thus Bryan prepared for 1896, when he would attempt to win the nomination as the party's candidate for the presidency.[23]

Given the fusionist tendencies in Nebraska, some people in the Farmers' Alliance doubted the effectiveness of maintaining the Alliance, and it was to those who feared and doubted that Kellie spoke in her speech. She addressed the issue of fusion as a destructive force within the Alliance, and she urged Alliance members to remember the bases of true Populism as chartered in the 1892 Omaha Platform: railroad reform, monetary reform, and land reform.

Kellie's speech moved her audience. Acknowledging the difficulty of their struggle for equality, she appealed to her listeners' religious convictions and desires to improve their troubled financial situations. She used Alliance goals spelled out in the Omaha Platform as a metaphor for "the promised land" and urged Alliance members to work for the benefit of their children.

> At times we grow weary and discouraged when we realize that the work of the Alliance is hardly begun, and that after the weary years of toil of the best men and women of the state we have hardly taken a step on the road to industrial freedom. We know that although we may not arrive there *our children will* enter into the promised land, and we can make their trials fewer and lighter, even if we live not to see the full light of freedom for mankind.

Continuing to use religious metaphors, Kellie exposed the hypocrisy of self-described Christians who actively watched while others suffered financial difficulties: "The Christian way . . . would soon right every legalized injustice, and yet the majority of the voters pretend to be his followers. Had they been so in deed and in truth how different would be the condition of our country." Kellie's purpose was to point out that government had not solved the problems of farmers and industrial workers. How could the Alliance members then give in to fusion when so little had been done?

Kellie went on to reiterate the main planks of the Omaha Platform. Farmers needed land reform, transportation reform, money reform, and the ability to directly vote on legislation. The Farmers' Alliance was the only way to achieve these political goals. In addition, she asked Alliance members if they wanted to rely on "the law-interpreting class" to educate the masses and to make people aware of Alliance goals: "A farmer can teach his brother farmers much better the principles of political economy and what he needs to better his condition than the most silvery-tongued office-seeking lawyer that ever lived in any party."[24] Kellie ended her speech with a newly composed poem also entitled "Stand up for Nebraska."

The speech was reprinted in at least three major newspapers, and Kellie enjoyed instant name recognition at the conference. As she modestly said in her political memoir, her address "seemed to have made a hit." By addressing the anxieties many Alliance members felt, Kellie gave renewed hope to those who had begun to doubt whether Populism in its Mid-Road form could make a difference. Her speech and song inspired people to act.

Women and Their Place in the Alliance

Because women did not generally speak publicly in the 1890s, Kellie's speech would have been quite extraordinary in any other major political party. When women were politically active, their activity was carried out in a female context. They worked on feminist issues such as suffrage or sought to use their "expertise" in the moral sphere to affect politics. Only a few progressive political groups in the 1890s encouraged women to participate in politics. Among them were the Greenback party, the Union Labor party, and the Farmers' Alliance. The Alliance allowed women to hold office within the party, and many women took advantage of the opportunity. The *Farmer's Wife,* a women's Alliance newspaper, estimated that twenty Alliance newspapers were edited by women and noted that women acted as traveling lecturers and held local offices in Alliance organizations.[25]

The Alliance was not completely egalitarian in nature, however, as Mary Jo Wagoner suggests in "Prairie Populists: Mary Lease and Luna Kellie." Wagoner comments that "Luna Kellie's activity probably more closely represents the majority of women who worked for the Alliance and Populist party during the 80s and 90s."[26] However, from the evidence I have uncovered it seems that Kellie was in fact unusual, relative to the average Populist woman, in starting a printing press and playing major roles in party politics, including a position as superintendent of public instruction in Omaha.

Not every politically active woman had a husband who supported her political activity or the literary means to accomplish the tasks she set for herself. It was the rare woman who held an office, drafted legislation, or spoke in public. Like Luna Kellie, women who fought on behalf of agrarian issues—issues men concerned themselves with—did not actively seek change in women's rights specifically. Advocates of women's suffrage who pushed Alliance members to support suffrage as an Alliance issue soon found that there were many men and some women who would not support a woman's right to vote even if the issue were politically expedient. Suffrage supporters learned that they would have to fight the battle on their own, without the support of men in any party.

Even activist women like Luna Kellie experienced second-class citizenship in the Alliance. She was not paid for her Alliance positions, even though her male counterparts received payment for their work. She stayed well within the "benevolent mother" role and worked to "bring better conditions for the coming generations" of farm families. While the Alliance offered a new forum for discussion that had not been previously open, there were clearly limitations on how much a woman could participate.

Kellie's Role as Alliance Secretary

As Kellie's political memoir makes clear, she accepted the office of secretary for the Nebraska Alliance with some ambivalence: "I was fairly dazed as I did not know whether I was capable of conducting the office or not. . . . my hands were very full and if I had extra time when others were asleep I would rather devote it to writing for the papers as I had been doing than to book-keeping." Her strong commitment to Alliance ideals led her to make the considerable sacrifices the position required of her and her family.

Kellie's secretarial responsibilities added long hours of work to her already busy schedule, as she arranged all the itineraries of Nebraska lecturers through daily correspondence. The family gave up a much-needed bedroom (there were then eight children in the household) and Kellie's sons made the ten-mile mail trips to deliver correspondence.

With no guidance from her predecessor or the executive committee, Kellie learned by doing, figuring out from her county records what past state Alliance secretaries had been interested in keeping. A harder job was coping with differing opinions among Alliance leaders about how money should be spent. When Kellie honored lecturer John H. Powers's request to have a thousand manuals printed she was "called down very promptly and hard by [the] President of [the] Executive Committee" and told not to spend any money without approval of the entire committee, whose members, Kellie notes with some irony, were "pretty well scattered over the state."

The spending issue that rankled most was that Kellie was never paid. Kellie mentions this no fewer than seven times in the ten pages of her political memoir, and it was obviously a great source of frustration to her. The primary reason for the lack of payment seems to have been the Alliance's serious financial situation. Whether committee members believed that Kellie should work without pay because she was a married woman is not known, but it is certainly a possibility—particularly because her predecessor, a single woman, was paid $8 per week. The only other person who did not receive a direct salary was John H. Powers. But his room and board were always paid by those around him, and he also managed to earn about $1.20 a day on the stump from donations of Alliance members and friends. Kellie's account of Powers's activities reveals some resentment: "he expected the Secretary to keep in daily touch arranging dates plan[ning] for route and finding friends to entertain and urging members in the vicinity to turn out etc." While Kellie did not overtly express her discontent to the members of the executive committee, she had a good idea of her economic value to the Alliance. She also accepted the fact that the Alliance was in such miserable financial shape that there was no money for her salary.

Kellie's Analysis of Alliance Problems

The problems in the Alliance that disturbed Kellie the most were the loss of grass-roots support and the general lack of unity and organization. When Kellie first went through the Alliance records, she was shocked to find a dramatic drop in participation in Alliance activities. The shock was even more severe because Kearney County had always had a deceivingly high rate of Alliance activity and participation relative to other areas of Nebraska because of the small but very enthusiastic group of Mid-Roaders in her area.

Kellie traced the spiral of Alliance participation by tracking the number of delegates represented at Nebraska Alliance meetings between the years 1889 and 1894. From a high of 900 delegates in 1890, the participation had dropped to 647 delegates in 1892 and to 76 delegates by 1894. The drop in Alliance support was symbolic of the nation's larger problems in 1894, when terrible conditions of drought and depression struck rural America. One might expect that membership in the Alliance would rise in a time of financial crisis, but it seems that many Alliance members were willing to support fusion candidates on the chance that they would be elected and ameliorate the farmers' condition.

Kellie saw the drop in participation as a sign that Alliance members were supporting William Jennings Bryan's Democratic-Populist fusion ticket instead of the Alliance. She also believed that people who had once been loyal to the Alliance were supporting the Populist party to the exclusion of state and local Alliance groups. She expressed the opinion that the Alliance had the best interest of the farmers in mind whereas the Populist party became increasingly vulnerable to fusion with Democrats.

Kellie Publishes a Mid-Road Paper

As the Nebraska Alliance had increasing difficulties obtaining dues from its members, Kellie and others on the executive committee "felt the need of direct communication with members so keenly" that the president and Luna Kellie were asked to study the idea of starting a state paper "if it [could] be done without debt to the Alliance."

Kellie hoped that a true Mid-Road Alliance newspaper could bring the farmers back together again and allow them to see the inherent problems with fusion. She took on the task of publishing a paper enthusiastically, realizing it was one of the Alliance's last hopes for reviving the Mid-Road philosophy in Nebraska. She even offered to assume the debt for publishing the paper during the first six months, a meaningful gesture given her family's financial situation.

Kellie sought advice from an Alliance branch in Denver, Colorado, whose state secretary, a man named Southworth, published a paper. After securing forty dollars from politicians "who owed their positions to the Alliance members,"[27] Kellie was able to publish the first and second editions of the *Wealth Makers*. The first paper was printed in July 1895.

Kellie juggled her professional and domestic roles, on press day letting her five-month-old daughter, Helen, play "in the waste basket" while she folded and addressed more than two thousand papers. Finally, to avoid the twelve-mile trip to the printer in Minden every month "come rain or shine," Kellie used advertising money advanced by her father to buy a printing press and learned to run it herself.

Originally the *Wealth Makers* did not have a high number of subscribers, and it seems Kellie received few responses to the many papers she sent out. In the spring of 1896 she began to publish the paper under the name the *Prairie Home*, and from this point on it seems to have been well organized and well received. The four- to eight-page *Prairie Home* (which the Nebraska State Historical Society has on microfilm for the years 1896 to 1901) appears professional and seems to have been effective in rallying support for the traditional Mid-Road Alliance stance. Every issue of the *Prairie Home* stated under the heading "Declaration of Purpose" the following resolution:

> Convinced that the farmers and laborers of this state will never secure "the establishment of right and justice to ourselves and our posterity" under a competitive system we therefore resolve: To labor for the establishment of a Co-operative Commonwealth. To do so we will endeavor to educate ourselves on co-operation, and will use our utmost efforts to establish co-operative industries of all kinds as object lessons.

Kellie's family members were instrumental in the success of the paper, which by 1899 had become a weekly. From her accounts, it appears that all members of her large family helped with production. Usually J.T. or one of the older boys inked the press, and the children always helped with preparation and distribution of the papers. On November 16, 1899, Kellie printed in the *Prairie Home* how that week's issue had been put together, giving the twentieth-century reader some insight into the process:

> This is strictly a woman's or rather a girl's paper this week. Mr. Kellie is away on business, and the boys having got our corn all cribbed are away helping others. The editor inks this week, so you know who to blame if you can hardly read your paper. Jessie runs the Washington press, Edith, Luna, and Lois (aged 10, 8, and 6) take turns "jogging" folding and wrapping. Baby Sophia got up to the case and "distributed"

an editorial, and if we ever get the paper done we will take it to a young Post-mistress to mail.

The significance of the family support Luna Kellie received should not be underestimated. Women's work was essential to running a farm, and women's work enabled men to participate in activities off the farm—particularly political activities. It is important to note that within some families who were active in the Alliance, the division of labor was directly affected by the political activity of women. In order for Kellie to travel, write, hold positions on boards, and edit the *Prairie Home*, she needed her husband and children to do the tasks for which she no longer had time.

Content of the *Prairie Home*

Kellie printed diverse articles from many of the larger reform press papers on Alliance topics, in addition to articles by Eugene Debs, Edward Bellamy, Elizabeth Cady Stanton, and other famous reformers. The *Prairie Home* always contained local Alliance news, calls to action, party platforms, and numerous letters to the editor. Some letters were lengthy analyses of articles or issues brought up in previous publications. Others were letters of praise or inspirational poems, and a very few were letters of criticism for the paper's strong Mid-Road stance. Kellie often contributed her own poems, and "My Prairie Home" later received wide distribution.

My Prairie Home

There's a dear old homestead on Nebraska's fertile plain
　　Where I toiled my manhood's strength away;
All that labor now is lost to me, but it is Shylock's gain,
　　For that dear old home he claims today.

Chorus
Ah, my dear prairie home! Nevermore in years to come
　　Can I call what I made by toil my own;
The railroads and banks combined, the lawyers paid to find
　　Out a way to rob me of my home.

It was many years ago that I first saw through this scheme,
　And I struggled from their meshes to get free;
But my neighbors all around me then were in a party dream,
　And they voted to rob my home from me.

Chorus
Now their homes are gone as well as mine, and they're awake
　at last,
　And they now see the great injustice done;
While some few their homes may save, yet the greater part,
　alas!
　Must be homeless for all time to come.

Chorus
We must now the robbers pay for a chance to till the soil,
　And when God calls us over the great range,
All a'heaven will be owned, I suppose, by men who never
　toil,
　So I doubt if we notice the exchange.

　　Kellie wrote various articles on local or national politics and
statements of purpose. Since she was involved in almost every
local Alliance organization, she could keep her readers abreast
of all local issues. She also covered urban industrial strikes, cases
of poverty, etc., in order to keep the rural farmers sympathetic
to urban industrial issues.
　　As one might expect, fusion was discussed at length in the
Prairie Home. The coverage included extensive examinations of
fusionists and fusionist strategy, along with attempts to keep
Alliance members in touch with current Middle-of-the-Road
counterstrategies against fusion. Kellie also kept her readers in
close contact with the southern element of the party, which had
a stronger cooperative movement than the Midwest did in the
late 1890s. When William Jennings Bryan visited Kentucky,
Kellie published in the November 28, 1899, issue an article by
Joe A. Parker, recording secretary-treasurer of the National Reform Press Association from Louisville, entitled "Bryan's Visit
to Kentucky." Parker, on behalf of the People's party in Kentucky, expressed the same contempt for Bryan's fusion politics

and for his betrayal of the Populist party, writing "Populists of the South will never support him again."

The letters, poems, and articles submitted by local and out-of-state readers made up the bulk of Kellie's paper. They are indicative of the widespread support her political stance had in Nebraska. Most letters were addressed "Dear Madam" or "Dear Mrs. Kellie" and went on to express support for the Mid-Road cause. Many wrote to affirm their support of different calls for reorganization of the Nebraska Alliance or to commend Kellie for articles written about the problems with fusion. For example, in the July 1897 issue Matilda Nagley wrote, "I have just received the Missouri World, and saw notice of your paper. Will say I am glad to see such a move by the ladies in the right direction. Will you please send me a sample copy of your paper? I may be able to assist you in some way. I am a TRUE BLUE Populist." Others wrote to vent their frustration about the weakness of the Alliance, as did M. H. Smith in the same July 1897 issue:

> Mrs. Kellie:
> Your paper received, also letter from others. Find enclosed 50 cents to pay for my paper. Our Alliance has been killed by fusion. The members becoming discouraged and heartsick, about as you express yourself. I stand and work in the "Middle of the road," from START TO FINISH, and can not believe that any fusionist is a true Populist. I can see no other way than that we must stand the oppression for another term and then others will have to fight the battle that should have been settled by us, and I believe could, had we kept out of FUSION.
> Respectfully, M. H. Smith

M. H. Smith's anxieties represent a growing sense of purposelessness that stemmed from fusion with the Democratic party in the national party conventions of 1896.

Kellie's contributions to the *Prairie Home* changed over the years. Her earlier poems were often filled with religious metaphors. As she became more involved in publishing the *Prairie Home* and more savvy about politics, she wrote fewer romantic poems and more pointed articles. She also participated more in

Mid-Road organizations, in the reform press, and in reorganizing her own Alliance chapter as an exclusively Mid-Road organization. Kellie became more convinced that the only remedy for the problems of political corruption was for the people to have a direct vote on legislation. Her politics increasingly focused on this issue. In the April 1898 issue of the *Prairie Home* Kellie wrote the following on behalf of the executive committee:

Call for a Meeting of the State Alliance

We the officers of the Nebraska Farmers Co-operative Alliance, having been requested by the Buffalo county Alliance to call a special meeting of the State Alliance to work in the interest of the middle-of-the-road Populist party of this state, and to devise plans to carry all the principles of the Omaha platform of the land, hereby request that members and former members who are opposed to fusion with either wing of plutocracy and will pledge themselves to stand by those, and those only who are sworn to enact ALL our principles into law, meet at Kearney on the 24th of May at 10:00 o'clock A.M. for the purpose of conference and re-organization.

The meeting had little attendance, except for Alliance members living in Buffalo County. Those involved agreed to call another meeting in Omaha on June 18, 1898, but as Kellie says in her political memoir, "this meeting did not materialize." Clearly, enthusiasm was waning for the Farmers' Alliance. Since Democrat William Jennings Bryan had been elected as the Populist candidate for president in 1896, many simply gave up on the Populist movement and the Farmers' Alliance. The fusion that took place at the convention of 1896 did indeed kill Populist morale in the Midwest. In the southern section, the Populists remained sworn enemies of Democrats, since they had endured extreme harassment and violence from Democratic forces in the South.[28]

Kellie's Disillusionment with Politics

By 1900 the paper had become increasingly dependent on local companies who wanted advertising space. Advertisements and fictional stories began to take more room in the paper, and local news began to be published before Alliance news. For example, the first page of the January 4, 1900, issue was filled with general news about a train crash, the latest market reports, a hanging, and other apolitical news. Originally the front page had covered Alliance news, and the paper itself had been devoted almost exclusively to Mid-Road, anti-fusion information.

On January 25, 1900, a discouraged Kellie made a public statement about her views on Populism. Convinced that the Populist party was no longer of any use to her fellow Alliance members, she had joined a new group called the Union Reform party, and she officially notified her readers that the *Prairie Home* had been "adopted as the official organ of the Union Reform Party in Kearney C[ounty]." Kellie reprinted an address she had delivered at the Union Reform party meeting:

> Like nearly all the members of the Alliance in this state and nation I was a Populist because that party was originated by Alliance men and women and delegates from other labor organizations. It was originally a labor party and its delegates were all delegates from labor organizations. When it ceased to be that, when it ceased advocating the principles of the Alliance and other labor organizations, when it accepted as delegates the attorneys of corporations and others of the worst enemies of labor, when it laughed our demands to scorn by declaring the land question immaterial and that the silver question was the money question I ceased to be a Populist just in proportion as they dropped out the principles of the Alliance and took upon themselves strange gods for "leaders." The eighteen years that have passed since I enlisted in the labor movement have served to enlighten my understanding of the needs of labor and intensify my devotion to the principles of the Alliance which I am more fully convinced than ever must be enacted into law before we will have "a government of the people, by the people and for the people." But I have given up all hope of the Populist party ever bringing any of them about. It has now so consolidated itself with one of the corrupt old political organizations that it no longer dares even to promise to enact any of them into

law. I fought this amalgamation from 1894 when it was first revealed to me by W. A. McKeighan until the past fall, when I considered the case hopeless and shall devote my time and strength hereafter to the Union Reform party which will give the people the right to vote directly on all law and hence the people can obtain any reform they are educated enough to desire.

Even though the Union Reform party garnered some support, the people involved were the same local activists who had participated in the Mid-Road Alliance, as Kellie had acknowledged in a December 7, 1899, article entitled "Without the Sacrifice of a Single Principle All Reforms Can Be Secured." There was no grass-roots support in Kellie's area for a new group to become established on any wide scale.

Moreover, the number of non-Alliance members subscribing to the *Prairie Home* continually increased. By October 25, 1901, Kellie no longer had the energy or the desire to publish a paper filled with advertisements and local news. Under the front-page banner she gave a terse statement: "This paper will appear as The Kearney County News next week." Kellie's political memoir makes clear her desperation and sadness on losing the paper: "We had hoped to bring better conditions for the coming generation and now knew that disorganized and discouraged as the old workers were there would have to be another generation grown to take up the work."

Reform Press Activities

Kellie was not the only publisher who experienced problems keeping her printing press operating in the 1890s. The Populist National Reform Press Association papers sought to educate people about the causes behind their suffering, wrought in large part by the depression that rocked the country in 1893. Lawrence Goodwyn comments in *Democratic Promise* that had "Populism been nothing else, the Reform Press Association could stand as a monument to the moral intensity of the agrarian crusade. The thunder of its great journals—*The Advocate, The American Nonconformist, The Appeal to Reason, The Southern Mer-*

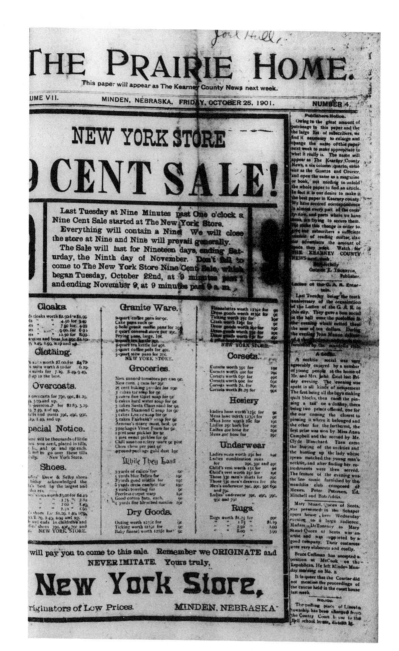

Last issue of the *Prairie Home*, October 25, 1901. Below the banner is Luna Kellie's announcement: "This paper will appear as The Kearney County News next week." Courtesy Nebraska State Historical Society.

cury, The People's Party Paper, and *The Progressive Farmer*—was echoed in literally thousands of tiny, struggling weeklies across the nation."[29]

Kellie's paper was one of the struggling weeklies, and Kellie herself was a member of the very dedicated reform press whose editors, Goodwyn says, were "a singular local level culmination of the American reforming instinct of the nineteenth century." The reform press fought for the Omaha Platform and criticized the kind of "democracy" in which entire governments could be bought by powerful captains of industry. The reform press succeeded in broadening the political debate that had been narrowed in the established press by the influence of big business. However, it was plagued by sectionalism between North and South, as Republicans urged their constituencies to "vote as they shot" in the Civil War, and by fusion candidates like William Jennings Bryan in Nebraska, whose motives were dubious. According to Goodwyn, fusion "offered to Bryan a fighting chance to avoid retirement."[30]

Bryan's success in manipulating the Democratic and Populist parties and finally securing both parties' presidential nomination in 1896 was a blow both to Mid-Road Populist morale and to the reform press. Most editors of small and large press agencies in Nebraska closed their printing presses when the Bryan fusion began. As Goodwyn put it, "reform press was kept alive by the faith of its editors and their willingness to work on a level of bare subsistence. When that faith was crushed by fusion they simply closed their papers."[31] Kellie, however, continued to publish until 1901, sustaining the hope that farmers might understand the inherent dangers of fusion.

Kellie's Final Word

In the late 1890s the chapter of the Nebraska State Alliance was faring no better than its paper, Kellie's *Prairie Home.* It was no longer able to pay national Alliance dues in 1898. The National Farmers' Alliance even changed its name in an attempt to recruit more members, and it loosened admission criteria to include anyone who was willing to pay dues. By 1899 the Nebraska Alliance was not functioning as a committee at all. In fact, when

Kellie was unable to attend the 1899 general meeting because of "sickness"—which in Kellie's terminology usually meant the birth of another child—the meeting seems not to have taken place at all. In her political memoir she notes, "no report was ever made to me as to what was done and the books were not returned. I never asked for them and do not know that a meeting was held. Think not, at least I was not told of any new election of officers."

Although there were no longer local Alliance meetings in which to participate, Kellie and her husband attended Middle-of-the-Road conventions in Cincinnati and in Grand Island, Nebraska. At the Cincinnati convention, Kellie met many of the members of the reform press who were responsible for the grass-roots Populists, and she remembered the meeting as "one of the pleasant memories of life." Kellie clearly enjoyed being around those who shared her political views, and even though many Nebraskans were not Mid-Roaders there was a significant minority who understood the dangers of compromising their political values by fusing with other parties.[32]

At the Grand Island convention the leaders of several Omaha labor unions requested that Kellie be nominated as the Omaha Alliance candidate for the position of Nebraska superintendent of public instruction. In her political memoir Kellie says, "This was an unexpected honor but accepted on urgent request of the Labor Unions of Omaha as they said they could get a larger vote for someone so well known." It would be interesting to explore further why a radical Middle-of-the-Roader like Kellie was recruited and elected if Nebraskans were as fusionist as Goodwyn suggests in Democratic Promise.[33]

After a brief period of activism as superintendent of public instruction, about which little information is available, Kellie seems to have slipped into near despair about the state of the Populist movement and the chances of the Alliance to make a comeback in any form. This despair was set off by the death of Asa Taylor, a good friend and active participant in the Alliance, whom Kellie describes as "the head and in fact nearly all of the Union Reform movement, [who] died from overwork."

By this time, Kellie notes, "Hardly a reform paper remained alive and the abuse [of the fusionists] was hard to bear."

Luna Kellie, ca. 1927, with great-great-granddaughters
Janice Moreland and Betty Lou Harris. Courtesy Nebraska
State Historical Society.

Selling the printing press was a strongly symbolic move for her.
She was "heartsick and discouraged . . . a physical wreck." She
had invested her money and time, as well as her heart and mind,
in the Farmers' Alliance, and now she "dared not even think of
what hopes we had had. It meant sleepless nights and nerves
completely unstrung."

Kellie was so disillusioned with the failure of Populism and
the Union Reform party to create any change in the political
landscape that she rejected thinking about politics at all: "I busy
myself with my garden and chickens and have given up all hope
of making the world any better." Perhaps the most heartrend-
ing statement of her utter despair are these words: "And so I
never vote."

Conclusion

Luna Kellie's experience in politics was sustained by hope: hope
that she could make life easier for her children, hope that she
could provide for her children and live on a farm, and hope that
she could change the system under which she lived. Kellie hung

on longer and fought harder than did many Populists and members of the Farmers' Alliance, and the realization that the reforms she supported would not take place may have been more difficult for her than for others.

Like many other women, Kellie hung on to the party because it was a chance to affect her destiny. Women lost more than men when they lost the Populist party and the Farmers' Alliance. They lost their marginal status as voters within the Populist party and the Alliance. No longer could they have a direct say in the workings of politics and the legislation that directly affected their lives and families. Once again, women were relegated to "influencing," and they would stay in that role for years to come.

Women like Luna Kellie did have an important effect within the Alliance structure and the household structure. Within the household, she alleviated her family's poverty and successfully provided the family with an income that supported the children, garden, and home. This was in addition to the duties of washing, cleaning, gardening, working in the fields, and raising children. Within the Alliance, she worked so that others would not have to experience the loss of children and land and the other hardships she had endured. She traveled, wrote, and became a well-known participant in public and political forums. In this way she expressed herself and gained the confidence that she was capable of significant political action. The fact that "there would have to be another generation grown to take up the work" does not diminish the importance or the success of Luna Kellie.

Notes

1. "Genealogy and History of the Family of Williams," MS3914, Farmers' Alliance Papers: Luna Kellie, Archives, Nebraska State Historical Society, Lincoln. This genealogy includes the ancestry of Luna Sanford's parents and a brief history of Luna and J. T. Kellie.

2. After the Civil War, monetary policies of the federal government and the banking industry deflated the dollar. The gov-

ernment needed to repay the banks around $450 million from greenback notes issued to fund the war. Since the banks expected 100-cent dollars in return for the 50-cent dollars they had bought, the government decided to hold the money supply at current levels while population and industrialization increased. The result was deflation of the dollar and lower prices for farming goods. See Lawrence Goodwyn, *Democratic Promise: The Populist Moment in America* (New York: Oxford University Press, 1976), pp. 4–24.

3. James C. Olson, *History of Nebraska* (Lincoln: University of Nebraska Press, 1955), p. 184.

4. The law was later ruled unconstitutional. See Addison E. Sheldon, *Nebraska: The Land and the People* (Chicago and New York: Lewis Publishing Company, 1931), p. 542.

5. Olson, p. 184.

6. Ibid., p. 213.

7. Ibid., p. 218.

8. Ibid., p. 223; Robert E. Riegel, "The Omaha Pool," *Iowa Journal of History and Politics* 22 (October 1924), 569–82; also see Ray H. Mattison, "The Burlington Tax Controversy in Nebraska over the Federal Land Grants," *Nebraska History* 28 (April–June 1947), 110–31.

9. Olson, p. 223; George W. Berge, *The Free Pass Bribery System* (Lincoln: Independent Publishing Company, 1905), p. 9.

10. Steven Jay Gould, author of *The Mismeasure of Man* (New York: W. W. Norton, 1981), comments that "no idea was ever more widely misused than Social Darwinism" as an excuse for explaining why the poor were poor. By definition, poor people were biologically incapable of doing any better. Gould writes that "for seventy years, under the sway of recapitulation scientists had collected data all loudly proclaiming the same message: adult blacks, women, and lower class whites [were] like upper class male children." Thus, they were inferior to any white adult upper-class male. See pp. 113, 124.

11. Barnes Grove Cass, *The Sod House* (Lincoln: University of Nebraska Press, 1930, 1970), p. 241.

12. Sheldon, p. 572.

13. Mari Sandoz, *Sandhill Sundays and Other Recollections* (Lincoln: University of Nebraska Press, 1970), p. 17.

14. Goodwyn defines "movement culture" as the process by

which farmers realized their oppression. "Applying the remedy" involved farmers' educating themselves and others, forming co-operatives to circumvent monopolies, and supporting traveling Farmers' Alliance lecturers. See pp. 160–61, 181–82, 210, 388–401, 426.

15. Ibid., p. 146, n. 47.

16. Sheldon, p. 688.

17. Ibid., pp. 688–89.

18. The year 1892 was momentous for the Populist party. When its national convention was held in Omaha in July, 12,000 Populists converged on the city, including famous reformers like Susan B. Anthony and Dr. Anna Shaw, who energetically called for women's suffrage. Delegates elected a president and created the so-called Omaha Platform, which promoted land reform, monetary reform, and railroad reform. Women's suffrage, however, was once again ignored, as it was in the Democratic and Republican parties. For more on the Omaha Platform, see Sheldon, pp. 716–17, and Goodwyn, pp. 593–96.

19. Goodwyn, pp. 239–42.

20. Ibid., p. 349.

21. Marilyn Dell Brady, "Populism and Feminism in a Newspaper by and for Women of the Kansas Farmers' Alliance 1891–1894," *Kansas History* 7, no. 4 (1984–1985), 286.

22. Jack S. Blocker, "The Politics of Reform: Populists, Prohibition, and Woman Suffrage 1891–1892," *Historian* 24, no. 4 (1972), 631.

23. Sheldon, pp. 741–48.

24. Kellie was referring to William Jennings Bryan, well known for his oratory and his support of free coinage of silver.

25. Brady, p. 283, n. 10.

26. In Karen Blair, ed., *Northwest Women's Heritage* (Seattle: Northwest Center for Research on Women, 1984), p. 208.

27. Senator W. V. Allen was a fusionist Democrat/Populist who was instrumental in getting William Jennings Bryan nominated for president in the 1896 Populist national convention. Governor Silas A. Holcomb, also a fusion proponent, was elected governor in 1894. See Goodwyn, pp. 219–20, 254, 256.

28. Ibid., p. 144.

29. Ibid., p. 354.

30. Ibid., p. 357.

31. Ibid., p. 493.

32. Goodwyn states in *Democratic Promise* that the term *Middle-of-the-Roader*, "of course, could not be used to describe the politics of the Shadow Movement in Nebraska—not even in 1892." The implication is that no one in Nebraska had an understanding of the meaning of the "real" Populist culture, which was characterized by collective and uncompromising action by allied farming people taken in their own best interest. While Goodwyn may be right about the political leaders of the state of Nebraska, there were many like the Kellies who understood the value of uncompromised Alliance demands. See p. 426.

33. Leaders like William Jennings Bryan were, of course, fusionists, but Goodwyn does not examine historical evidence about lower-level party members from the inside out, particularly in Nebraska. See p. 390.

★ SELECTED BIBLIOGRAPHY ★

Alliance Independent. Microfilm. Nebraska State Historical Society, Lincoln.

Bakken, Douglas. "Luna E. Kellie and the Farmers' Alliance." *Nebraska History* 50 (1986).

Berge, George W. *The Free Pass Bribery System.* Lincoln: Independent Publishing Company, 1905.

Blocker, Jack S. "The Politics of Reform: Populists, Prohibition, and Woman Suffrage 1891–1892." *Historian* 24, no. 4 (1972).

Brady, Marilyn Dell. "Populism and Feminism in a Newspaper by and for Women of the Kansas Farmers' Alliance 1891–1894." *Kansas History* 7, no. 4 (1984–1985).

Cass, Barnes Grove. *The Sod House.* Lincoln: University of Nebraska Press, 1930, 1970.

Cherny, Robert. *Populism, Progressivism, and the Transformation of Nebraska Politics 1889–1915.* Lincoln: University of Nebraska Press, 1981.

Farmers' Alliance Papers: Luna Kellie. Archives. Nebraska State Historical Society, Lincoln.

Fink, Deborah. *Open Country Iowa: Rural Women, Tradition, and Change.* New York: State University of New York Press, 1986.

Goodwyn, Lawrence. *Democratic Promise: The Populist Moment in America.* New York: Oxford University Press, 1976.

Gould, Steven Jay. *The Mismeasure of Man.* New York: W. W. Norton, 1981.

Jensen, Joan. *Loosening the Bonds: Mid-Atlantic Farm Women 1750–1850.* New Haven and London: Yale University Press, 1986.

Mattison, Ray H. "The Burlington Tax Controversy in Nebraska over the Federal Land Grants." *Nebraska History* 28 (1947).

Olson, James C. *History of Nebraska*. Lincoln: University of Nebraska Press, 1955.

Ostler, Jeffrey D. "The Fate of Populism: Agrarian Radicalism and State Politics in Kansas, Nebraska, and Iowa, 1880–1892. Ph.D. dissertation, University of Iowa, 1990.

Prairie Home. Microfilm. Nebraska State Historical Society, Lincoln.

Riegel, Robert E. "The Omaha Pool." *Iowa Journal of History and Politics* 22 (1924).

Sandoz, Mari. *Sandhill Sundays and Other Recollections*. Lincoln: University of Nebraska Press, 1970.

Sheldon, Addison E. *Nebraska: The Land and the People*. Chicago and New York: Lewis Publishing Company, 1931.

Wagoner, Mary Jo. "Prairie Populists: Mary Lease and Luna Kellie." In Karen Blair, ed., *Northwest Women's Heritage*. Seattle: Northwest Center for Research on Women, 1984.

OTHER SINGULAR LIVES